C Programming for the Absolute Beginner, Third Edition

Keith Davenport

Michael Vine

Cengage Learning PTR

CENGAGE
Learning·

Professional · Technical · Reference

Australia, Brazil, Japan, Korea, Mexico, Singapore, Spain, United Kingdom, United States

CENGAGE
Learning®
Professional • Technical • Reference

C Programming for the Absolute Beginner, Third Edition
Keith Davenport and Michael Vine

Publisher and General Manager, Cengage Learning PTR:
Stacy L. Hiquet

Associate Director of Marketing:
Sarah Panella

Manager of Editorial Services:
Heather Talbot

Senior Product Manager:
Mitzi Koontz

Project Editor/Copy Editor:
Karen A. Gill

Interior Layout:
Shawn Morningstar

Cover Designer:
Mike Tanamachi

Indexer:
Sharon Shock

Proofreader:
Sam Garvey

For product information and technology assistance, contact us at
Cengage Learning Customer & Sales Support, 1-800-354-9706

For permission to use material from this text or product, submit all requests online at **cengage.com/permissions**

Further permissions questions can be emailed to **permissionrequest@cengage.com**

Microsoft, Windows, and Internet Explorer are either registered trademarks or trademarks of Microsoft Corporation in the United States and/or other countries. The Cygwin DLL and utilities are Copyright 2013 Red Hat, Inc. UNIX is a registered trademark of the Open Group in the United States and other countries.

All other trademarks are the property of their respective owners.

All images © Cengage Learning unless otherwise noted.

Library of Congress Control Number: 2014945699
ISBN-13: 978-1-305-27376-4
ISBN-10: 1-305-27376-1

Cengage Learning PTR
20 Channel Center Street
Boston, MA 02210
USA

Cengage Learning is a leading provider of customized learning solutions with office locations around the globe, including Singapore, the United Kingdom, Australia, Mexico, Brazil, and Japan. Locate your local office at: **international.cengage.com/region**

Cengage Learning products are represented in Canada by Nelson Education, Ltd.

For your lifelong learning solutions, visit **cengageptr.com**.

Visit our corporate Web site at **cengage.com**.

Printed in the United States of America
2 3 4 5 6   22 21 20 19 18

To my mother, Amy, whose belief in me carries me to this day.

—Keith Davenport

Acknowledgments

In order for a book to make it from the word processor to your shelf, a symphony of talented players must play their parts with precision, timing, and skill. When those players are also professional, kind, and dedicated, it elevates the experience for both the players and the audience. I am grateful for Mitzi Koontz, Karen Gill, and Michael Vine for sharing their talents and allowing me to help produce this edition of *C Programming for the Absolute Beginner*. It was a privilege to work with each of you. Thank you also to this edition's proofreader, Sam Garvey, for going beyond the call of duty and making some excellent corrections.

About the Authors

Keith Davenport is an industry jack-of-all trades who has worked in publishing, media, and technology for more than 20 years. Outside the industry, he has been a film writer and producer and has served various in-need populations as a social worker.

Michael Vine is a senior IT professional who specializes in data warehousing and business intelligence. Beyond corporate life, he has taught computer science classes at the university and college level and authored many software programming books.

Table of Contents

2

3

4

Looping Structures 79

5

Structured Programming 107

6

7

8

Strings 171

9

Introduction to Data Structures 193

10

11

12

F

Introduction

C is a powerful procedural-based programming language developed in 1972 by Dennis Ritchie within the halls of Bell Telephone Laboratories. The C programming language was originally developed for use with the UNIX platform and has since spread to many other systems and applications. C has influenced a number of other programming languages, including C++ and Java.

Beginning programmers, especially those enrolled in computer science and engineering majors, need to build a solid foundation of operating systems, hardware, and application development concepts. Numerous learning institutions accomplish this by teaching their students how to program in C so that they may progress to advanced concepts and other languages built upon C.

Many students of C will rightly admit that it's not an easy language to learn, but the professional insight, clear explanations, examples, and pictures in the Cengage Learning *for the Absolute Beginner* series make learning C easy and fun. Each chapter contains programming challenges, a chapter review, and a complete program that uses chapter-based concepts to construct an easily built application.

To work through this book in its entirety, you should have access to a computer with a C compiler such as gcc (see Chapter 1) or TCC (see Appendix D) and at least one text editor. On UNIX or in an emulated environment, you might have vi, Vim, Pico, nano, or Emacs. Under Microsoft Windows, you might use Notepad or any other plain-text editor.

What You'll Find in This Book

To learn how to program a computer, you must acquire a progression of skills. If you have never programmed at all, you will probably find it easiest to go through the chapters in order. Programming is not a skill you can learn by reading. You have to write programs to learn. This book has been designed to make the process reasonably painless and hopefully fun.

Each chapter begins with a brief introduction to chapter-based concepts. Once inside the chapter, you'll look at a series of programming concepts and small programs that illustrate each of the major points of the chapter. Finally, you'll put these concepts together to build a complete program at the end of the chapter. All the programs are short enough that you can type them in yourself (which is a great way to look closely at code), but they are also available via the publisher's website (www.cengageptr.com/downloads). Located at the end of every chapter is a summary that outlines key concepts learned. Use the summaries to refresh your memory on important concepts. In addition to summaries, each chapter contains programming challenges that will help you learn and cement chapter-based concepts.

Throughout the book, I'll throw in a few other tidbits, notably the following:

Trick

These contain information that deserves extra attention.

Trap

These warn or caution when it's easy to make a mistake or where you might run into a problem.

Hint

These provide additional insight or information related to a chapter topic.

SIDEBAR

As you examine concepts in this book, I'll show you how the concepts are used beyond beginning programming or in the real world.

Who This Book Is For

This book was designed with the absolute beginner in mind. It is not for experienced C programmers wanting to learn object-oriented programming (OOP) with C++ or advanced C data structures, such as linked lists.

This book is for you if

- You're a college or high school student studying beginning programming with C.
- You're an experienced programmer in other high-level languages, such as Visual Basic, VBA, HTML, or JavaScript, and you are looking to add C to your repertoire.
- You're a programming hobbyist/enthusiast looking to learn C on your own.
- You're interested in learning C++, C#, or Java and you were told to learn C first.
- You've always wanted to learn how to program and have chosen C as your first language.

If you fall into any of the preceding categories, you will enjoy this book's nonintimidating approach to programming in C. Specifically, I will teach you the basics of C programming using nongraphical text editors and the ANSI C compiler gcc. You will learn fundamental programming concepts such as variables, conditions, loops, arrays, structures, and file I/O that can be useful in learning any programming language. Of course, you will also learn some C-specific topics such as pointers and dynamic memory allocation, which make the C language unique and powerful.

Companion Website Downloads

This book has a companion website where you can find all the complete chapter programs. You may download the companion website files from www.cengageptr.com/downloads.

1

Getting Started with C Programming

Welcome to *C Programming for the Absolute Beginner, Third Edition*! The C programming language is an excellent foundation on which to build your programming career or hobby. Whether you're a computer technology student, a self-taught programmer, or a seasoned software engineer, learning C gives you conceptual knowledge and practical skills that will serve you well in understanding many other computer subjects, including operating system concepts, memory management, and other high-level programming languages.

Throughout this book, I guide you through a series of examples designed to teach you the basics of C programming. I assume you have no prior experience with C programming or beginning computer science concepts. There are no prerequisites for this book (including advanced math concepts), although I do assume that you have a basic understanding of at least one Microsoft or UNIX-based (or Linux-based) operating system and that you know how to use a text editor.

If you already have some prior programming experience with other languages, such as Java, Visual Basic, Ruby, PowerBuilder, or Python, you will still benefit from this book. I hope after reading *C Programming for the Absolute Beginner, Third Edition* you will continue to find this text a useful C programming reference.

I cover the following topics in this chapter:

- Installing and configuring the Cygwin environment
- Understanding the `main()` function
- Using comments
- Understanding keywords
- Working with program statements
- Using directives
- Creating and running your first C program
- Debugging C programs

Installing and Configuring the Cygwin Environment

All you need to learn how to program in C is access to a computer, a text editor, C libraries, and a C compiler. Throughout this book, I use a simple text editor to write C programs. Unlike many high-level programming languages (such as Visual Basic or C#), the C language doesn't require a high-end graphical user interface (GUI). In fact, a complex and feature-rich interface can be distracting for a beginner who wants to learn programming. It's easy to focus on the bells and whistles of a fancy interface instead of the underlying programming concepts, such as variables and loops, which should be the *primary* concern for the beginning programmer.

> **Hint**
>
> You know what a computer is and what a text editor is, but what is a C library? What is a C compiler? Both are explained later in this chapter, but in short, a *library* is prewritten code that you use to perform certain standard functions, such as getting input from a user. A *compiler*, such as gcc, is a program that takes the code you enter into a text file and converts it into a format that computers can use and creates an executable program.

There are several free C compilers and text editors that you can use. Of course, there are many commercial ones, too. If you already have access to the necessary programming tools, you can skip this installation section. But if not, my clever friends at Cygwin have developed a simple, yet robust Linux-like environment for Windows that includes many free software packages, such as a C compiler called gcc, text editors, and other common utilities. You can download Cygwin's free software components from www.cygwin.com.

The Cygwin setup process is simple, but if you have questions or issues, you can visit the online user guide at http://cygwin.com/cygwin-ug-net/cygwin-ug-net.html. Once you've installed Cygwin, you have access to many UNIX-based utilities via a UNIX shell or the Windows command prompt.

A minimum of 400MB of free hard drive space is required for installation (more or less depending on the components selected). To install Cygwin and its associated components, download the setup file from http://cygwin.com/install.html. Follow the setup screens until you get to the Cygwin Setup—Select Packages window. Once there, you can select the components you want to install. The default components selected plus the "gcc-core: C Compiler" installation component are enough to enable you to work through all the code in this book. The gcc-core: C Compiler component is not selected by default, however. To select this component, click the plus sign (+) next to the Devel category and scroll down until you find the gcc-core: C Compiler component. Click the word Skip to select the component for installation.

Trick

If you want to use a text editor within Cygwin, go to the Editors section and select Nano (covered in Appendix C, "nano Quick Guide"), Vim (covered in Appendix B, "Vim Quick Guide"), or both. You can also create your code outside of Cygwin in a text editor such as Notepad.

Note that the installer may prompt you to install other packages to resolve dependencies. If so, allow the installer to include those packages as well.

After successfully installing the Cygwin environment, you will have access to an emulated UNIX (Linux) operating system through a UNIX shell. To start the UNIX shell, simply find the Cygwin shortcut located on the desktop or through the program group found in the Start menu.

After you start the program, the Cygwin UNIX shell should resemble Figure 1.1.

Note the syntax used for the UNIX command prompt in Figure 1.1. Yours will differ.

```
Keith@Keith-DesktopPC   ~
$
```

Figure 1.1
Launching the Cygwin UNIX shell.

The first line shows the user who is logged into the UNIX shell (which is the user logged into the computer you are using—in my case, Keith) and the name of that computer. (Keith-DesktopPC is the very creative name of my PC.) The next line starts with a dollar sign ($). This is the UNIX command prompt from which you enter and execute UNIX commands.

Depending on your specific installation (Cygwin version) and configuration (components selected) of Cygwin, you may need to have Cygwin's bin directory added to your system's PATH environment variable. If you installed the 32-bit version of Cygwin, use the following:

```
c:\cygwin\bin
```

If you installed the 64-bit version of Cygwin, however, use this instead:

```
c:\cygwin64\bin
```

> **Trick**
>
> For the sake of brevity, I'm going to assume that you installed the 32-bit version of Cygwin. If you do have the 64-bit version of Cygwin, which is perfectly fine, substitute c:\cygwin64 for c:\cygwin whenever the file path is referenced in this book.

Cygwin and other programs use the PATH environment variable to find executable files to run. If you are using a Microsoft-based operating system, you can edit the PATH variable in a couple of ways. One trick is to launch a Microsoft-based command shell (DOS window) by typing the keyword cmd from the Run dialog box accessed via the Start menu. From the c:\ prompt (in the command shell), type the following:

```
set PATH=%PATH%;c:\cygwin\bin
```

This command appends c:\cygwin\bin to the end of the current PATH variable without overwriting it. To verify that the command was successful, simply type the keyword PATH from the same Microsoft-based command shell window. Note that a semicolon separates each distinct directory structure in the PATH's value. If necessary, consult your system's documentation for more information on environment variables and specifically updating the PATH system variable.

Understanding the main() Function

This section starts with the beginning of every C program: the main() function. First, however, I want to explain metaphorically what a function is. From a programming perspective, *functions* enable you to group a logical series of activities, or *program statements*, under one name. For example, suppose you want to create a function called bakeCake.

An algorithm for baking a cake might look like this:

> Mix wet ingredients in mixing bowl
> Combine dry ingredients
> Spoon batter into greased baking pan
> Bake cake at 350 degrees for 30 minutes

Note that giving your functions descriptive names helps anyone reading your code—even you at a later date when memory fades—understand what the function is supposed to accomplish.

Functions are typically not static, meaning they are living and breathing entities, again metaphorically, that take in and pass back information. Thus, my bakeCake function would take in a list of ingredients to bake (called *parameters*) and return a finished cake (called a *value*).

The main() function is like any other programming function in that it groups like activities and can take in parameters (information) and pass back values (again, information). What makes the main() function different from other functions is that it returns values to the operating system, whereas other functions that you use and create in this book return values to the calling C statement inside the main() function.

In this book, I use main() functions that do not take parameters from the operating system and only return a value of 0.

ALGORITHMS

An *algorithm* is a step-by-step process or a set of rules for solving a problem. An algorithm can be as simple as a recipe to bake a cake or as complicated as the process to implement an autopilot system for a 747 jumbo jet.

Algorithms usually begin with a problem statement or question. (Cake sounds good. How can I create and bake a cake?) As a programmer, before you write any code, you take this problem and break it down into the steps for solving it. Once you have this list of steps as a guide, you can begin the actual coding.

Trick

Although programs automatically return a value of 0 to the calling program (in this case, the operating system) when the program completes without error, many programmers consider it good practice to have the main() function explicitly return a value of 0 to indicate successful execution. Examples in this book follow this practice, which becomes useful when you begin to write more advanced programs that have the main() function return values other than 0 to indicate various error conditions.

```
int main()
{
    return 0;
}
```

As the preceding example shows, the main() function begins with the keywords int and main, followed by two empty parentheses (). This tells the computer that this is a function called "main," and it returns an integer (int) value to the operating system. If a function is passed values, which are called *arguments* or *parameters*, the parentheses delineate the types of parameters that the function accepts. As noted, the main() functions created in this book do not use function parameters, so the parentheses are empty.

Trap

C is a case-sensitive programming language. For example, the function names main(), Main(), and MAIN() are *not* the same. Incidentally, it takes extra computing resources to *not* be case-sensitive, because input devices such as keyboards distinguish between cases.

Following the parentheses are two curly braces. The first brace denotes the beginning of a logical programming block, and the last brace denotes the end of a logical programming block. Each function implementation requires that you use a beginning brace ({) and a closing brace (}).

The following program code demonstrates a complete, albeit simple, C program. From this code, you learn how single program statements come together to form a complete C program. Programming books traditionally call the first program Hello, World, but I'm going to break with convention and call mine C You Later, World.

```
/* C Programming for the Absolute Beginner */
#include <stdio.h>

int main()
{
    printf("\nC you later\n");
    return 0;
}
```

When the preceding program is compiled and run, it outputs the text C you later to the computer screen, as shown in Figure 1.2.

Review the sample program code in Figure 1.3; you can see the many components that comprise a small C program.

The remainder of this chapter covers these components and the way each is used to build a simple C program.

Figure 1.2
The output of a simple C program.

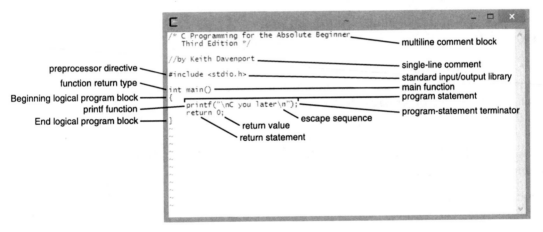

Figure 1.3 The building blocks of a simple C program.

Using Comments

Comments are an integral part of program code in any programming language. Comments help to identify program purpose and explain complex routines. They are valuable to you as the programmer and to other programmers looking at your code.

In the following line of code, the compiler ignores the text C Programming for the Absolute Beginner because it is delineated with the characters /* and */.

```
/* C Programming for the Absolute Beginner */
```

The characters /* signify the beginning of a comment block, and the characters */ signify the end of a comment block. These characters do not need to be on the same line and can be used to create both single-line and multiline comments. The following block of code shows multiline commenting:

```
/*  C Programming for the Absolute Beginner
    Chapter 1 - Getting Started with C Programming
*/
```

Your C program either won't compile or won't compile correctly if you omit one of the comment character sets or you reverse the characters. For example, the following code segment omits one of the comment character sets and does not compile:

```
/* C Programming for the Absolute Beginner
```

The next line of code also does not compile because comment characters have been incorrectly ordered:

```
*/ C Programming for the Absolute Beginner */
```

Trick

If you have trouble remembering the proper order of the comment characters, you can visualize them as two people using a bat to hit a ball toward each other. The bat (/) needs to hit the ball (*) toward the other bat and not away from it.

If your comment does not need to span multiple lines, you have the option of simply preceding the comment with a double forward slash (//), as shown here:

```
//by Keith Davenport
```

Trap

If your C compiler supports C++, which gcc does, you can use the single line // character set for one-line commenting. Be aware that not all C compilers support the single-line character set.

The compiler ignores any characters read after the characters // for that line only. You can still create a multiline comment block with //, but you need the slashes in front of each line in the block. For example, the following code creates a multiline comment block:

```
//C Programming for the Absolute Beginner
//Chapter 1 - Getting Started with C Programming
//by Keith Davenport
```

Understanding Keywords

There are 32 words defined as keywords in the standard ANSI C programming language. These keywords have predefined uses and cannot be used for any other purpose in a C program. The compiler—in this case gcc—uses these keywords as an aid to building the program. Note that you must always write these keywords in lowercase (see Table 1.1).

Be aware that in addition to the list of keywords in Table 1.1, your C language compiler may define more. If it does, you'll find them listed in the documentation that came with your compiler.

As you progress through this book, I will show you how to use many of the aforementioned C language keywords.

TABLE 1.1 C LANGUAGE KEYWORDS

Keyword	Description
auto	Defines a local variable as having a local lifetime
break	Passes control out of the programming construct
case	Branch control
char	Basic data type
const	Defines a value that cannot be modified
continue	Passes control to loop's beginning
default	Branch control
do	do while loop
double	Floating-point data type
else	Conditional statement
enum	Defines a group of constants of type int
extern	Indicates an identifier as defined elsewhere
float	Floating-point data type
for	for loop
goto	Transfers program control unconditionally
if	Conditional statement
int	Basic data type
long	Type modifier
register	Stores the declared variable in a CPU register

TABLE 1.1 C LANGUAGE KEYWORDS (CONTINUED)

Keyword	Description
return	Exits the function
short	Type modifier
signed	Type modifier
sizeof	Returns expression or type size
static	Preserves variable value after its scope ends
struct	Groups variables into a single record
switch	Branch control
typedef	Creates a new type
union	Groups variables that occupy the same storage space
unsigned	Type modifier
void	Empty data type
volatile	Allows a variable to be changed by a background routine
while	Repeats program execution while the condition is true

Working with Program Statements

Many lines in C programs are considered *program statements*, which serve to control program execution and functionality. Many of these program statements must end with a statement terminator. In C, a *statement terminator* is a semicolon (;). The following line of code, which includes the printf() function, demonstrates a program statement with a statement terminator:

```
printf("\nC you later\n");
```

The following are some common program statements that do not require the use of statement terminators:

- Comments
- Preprocessor directives (which are explained later in this chapter, such as #include or #define)
- Begin and end program block identifiers
- Function definition beginnings (for example, main())

The preceding program statements don't require the semicolon (;) terminator because they are not executable C statements or function calls. Only C statements that perform work during program execution require the semicolons.

A function commonly used for displaying output to the computer screen is printf(). As shown next, you use the printf() function to write the text C you later to the standard output (demonstrated in Figure 1.2):

```
printf("\nC you later\n");
```

Like most functions, the printf() function takes a value as a parameter. (I'll talk more about functions in Chapter 5, "Structured Programming.") You must enclose in quotation marks any text you want to display in the standard output.

For the most part, characters or text that you want to appear onscreen are put inside quotation marks, with the exception of escape characters or escape sequences. The backslash character (\) is the *escape character*. When you execute the printf() statement shown earlier, the program looks forward to the next character that follows the backslash. In this case, the next character is the character n. Together, the backslash (\) and n characters make up an *escape sequence*.

Hint

Escape sequences are special characters in strings that enable you to communicate with a display device or printer and send control characters to specify actions such as forcing a new line (\n) or making a horizontal tab (\t).

This particular escape sequence (\n) tells the program to add a new line. Take a look at the following program statement. How many new lines are added to standard output with this one printf() function?

```
printf("\nC you later\n");
```

This printf() function adds two new lines for formatting purposes. Before any text is shown, the program outputs a new line. After the text is written to standard output, in this case the computer screen, another new line is written.

Table 1.2 describes some common escape sequences.

TABLE 1.2 COMMON ESCAPE SEQUENCES

Escape Sequence	Purpose
\n	Creates a new line
\t	Moves the cursor to the next tab
\r	Moves the cursor to the beginning of the current line
\\	Inserts a backslash
\"	Inserts a double quote
\'	Inserts a single quote

Escape Sequence \n

As depicted in Figures 1.4 and 1.5, you can use escape sequence \n in a multitude of ways to format output.

The following code segment generates three separate lines with only one `printf()` function:

```
printf("line1\nline2\nline3\n");
```

The next code segment demonstrates how you can use escape sequence \n with multiple `printf()` statements to create a single line of output:

```
printf("C ");
printf("for the ");
printf("Absolute Beginner\n");
```

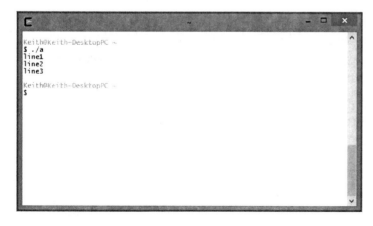

Figure 1.4
Using escape sequence \n with one printf() function to generate multiple lines.

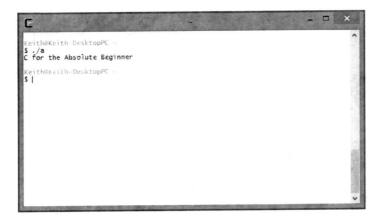

Figure 1.5
Using escape sequence \n with multiple printf() functions to generate a single line.

Escape Sequence \t

Escape sequence \t moves the cursor to the next tab space. This escape sequence is useful for formatting output in many ways. For example, a common formatting desire is to create columns in your output, as the following program statements demonstrate:

```
printf("\nSun\tMon\tTue\tWed\tThu\tFri\tSat\n");
printf("\t\t\t\t1\t2\t3\n");
printf("4\t5\t6\t7\t8\t9\t10\n");
printf("11\t12\t13\t14\t15\t16\t17\n");
printf("18\t19\t20\t21\t22\t23\t24\n");
printf("25\t26\t27\t28\t29\t30\t31\n");
```

As shown in Figure 1.6, the preceding program statements create formatted columns that display a sample calendar month.

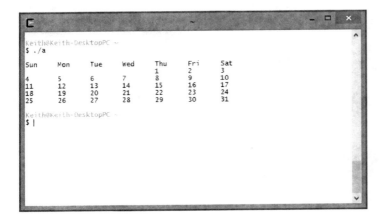

Figure 1.6
Demonstrating the use of tab spaces and columns with escape sequence \t.

Escape Sequence \r

You may find the escape sequence \r useful for some formatting tasks when the cursor's position is important, especially with printed output, because a printer can overwrite text that is already printing. The following program code demonstrates how it works; the output is shown in Figure 1.7:

```
printf("This escape sequence moves the cursor ");
printf("to the beginning of this line\r");
```

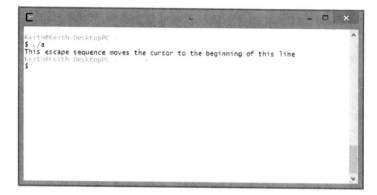

Figure 1.7
Demonstrating escape sequence \r.

Escape Sequence \\

Escape sequence \\ inserts a backslash into your text. This may seem unnecessary at first, but remember that whenever the program reads a backslash in a printf() function, it expects to see a valid escape character right after it. In other words, the backslash character (\) is a special character in the printf() function; if you need to display a backslash in your text, you must use this escape sequence. The following program statement demonstrates escape sequence \\. The output is shown in Figure 1.8:

```
printf("c:\\cygwin\\bin must be in your system path");
```

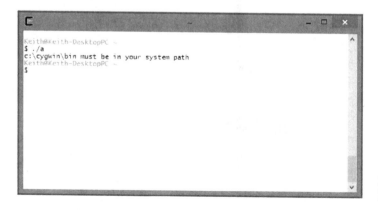

Figure 1.8
Demonstrating escape sequence \\.

Escape Sequence \"

Another reserved character in the printf() function is the double quote (") character. To insert a quote into your outputted text, use the escape sequence \" as demonstrated in the following program statement. The output is shown in Figure 1.9:

```
printf("\"This is quoted text\"");
```

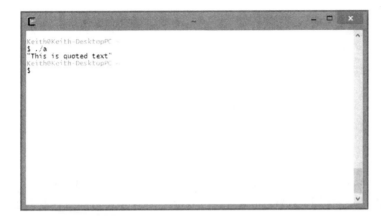

Figure 1.9
Creating quotes with escape sequence \".

Escape Sequence \'

Similar to the double quote escape sequence (\") is the single quote (also called an apostrophe) escape sequence (\'). To insert a single quote into your outputted text, use the escape sequence \' as demonstrated in the following program statement and in Figure 1.10:

```
printf("\nA single quote looks like \'\n");
```

Figure 1.10
Inserting single quotes
with escape sequence \'.

Using Directives

Here's another look at the sample program shown earlier in the chapter:

```
/* C Programming for the Absolute Beginner */
//by Michael Vine and Keith Davenport
#include <stdio.h>

int main()
{
    printf("\nC you later\n");
    return 0;
}
```

Notice the program statement that begins with the pound sign (#):

```
#include <stdio.h>
```

When the C preprocessor encounters the pound sign, it performs certain actions depending on the directive that occurs prior to compiling. In the preceding example, I told the preprocessor to include the stdio.h library with my program.

The name stdio.h is short for *standard input output header file*. It contains links to various standard C library functions, such as printf(). Excluding this preprocessor directive does not have an adverse effect when compiling or running your program. However, including the header file allows the compiler to better help you determine error locations. You should always add a directive to include any library header files that you use in your C programs.

In the chapters to come, you will learn other common library functions, how to use preprocessor directives such as macros, and how to build your own library files.

Creating and Running Your First C Program

The gcc compiler is an ANSI standard C compiler. A C program goes through a lot of steps prior to becoming a running or executing program. The gcc compiler performs a number of tasks for you. Most notable are the following:

- Preprocesses the program code and looks for various directives
- Generates error codes and messages, if applicable
- Compiles program code into an object code and stores it temporarily on disk
- Links any necessary library to the object code, creates an executable file, and stores it on disk

Hint

ANSI is an abbreviation for the *American National Standards Institute*. ANSI's common goal is to provide computing standards for people who use information systems.

Use the .c extension when creating and saving C programs. This extension is the standard naming convention for programs created in C. To create a new C program, run a text editor such as Notepad from Windows, or use nano or Vim as shown here:

```
nano hello.c
vim hello.c
```

Trick

nano is another common UNIX-based text editor that comes with the Cygwin software package. From an end user perspective, it is much more intuitive and easier to use than Vim, but it does not have Vim's degree of functionality. Though not selected in a default installation of Cygwin, nano and other text editors can be selected during installation via the Select Packages window under the Editors section.

Both of the preceding command statements open a text editor and create a new file called hello.c.

Once you've created and saved a C program using an editor such as nano or Vim, you are ready to compile your program using gcc.

From the Cygwin UNIX shell, type the following:

```
gcc hello.c
```

If your program compiles successfully, gcc creates a new executable file called a.exe.

Trap

If you are unsuccessful in running your compiled program, verify that the %systemdrive%:\ cygwin\bin (where %systemdrive% is the drive where Cygwin is installed) directory structure has been added to your system path variable.

a.exe is the default name for all C programs compiled with this version of gcc. If you're programming under a different version of gcc on a UNIX operating system, the filename may be a.out.

Every time you compile a C program with gcc, it overwrites the previous data contained in the a.exe file. You can correct this by giving gcc an option to specify a unique name for your executable file. The syntax for specifying a unique executable name follows:

gcc programName **-o** executableName

The programName keyword is the name of your C program, the -o (letter o) option tells gcc that you will specify a unique compile name, and the executableName keyword is the desired output name. Here's another example that uses actual filenames:

```
gcc hello.c -o hello.exe
```

You can find a wealth of information on the gcc program by accessing gcc's man pages (the online manual pages for UNIX commands) from the UNIX prompt as shown here:

```
man gcc
```

To execute your program from the Cygwin UNIX prompt, type the following:

```
./hello
```

Unlike Windows, the UNIX shell does not by default look in the current directory when trying to execute a program. By preceding the name of your compiled program with the ./ character sequence, you're telling the UNIX shell to look for the compiled C program, in this case hello, in the current directory.

If you're using a Microsoft Windows system, you can also execute your program from a Microsoft-based command shell often referred to as a DOS prompt (provided you're in the working directory) by simply typing in the name of the program.

Note that it is not necessary to follow the compiled program name with the file extension .exe in either case.

Debugging C Programs

If your program compiles, exits, or executes abnormally, there is almost certainly an error (a *bug*) in your program. You'll spend a fair amount of your programming time finding and removing these bugs. This section offers some tips to help you get started. Remember, though, that debugging is as much art as it is computer science and, of course, the more you practice programming, the easier debugging will become! Often a program compiles and executes just fine but produces results you did not expect or want. For example, the following program—and its output, shown in Figure 1.11—compiles and executes without error, but the output is unreadable, or in other words, not what I expected.

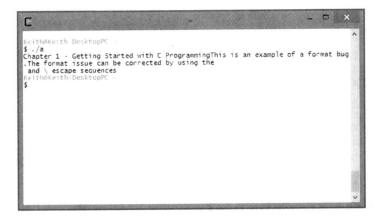

Figure 1.11
Error in formatting.

```c
#include <stdio.h>

int main()
{
    printf("Chapter 1 - Getting Started with C Programming");
    printf("This is an example of a format bug.");
    printf("The format issue can be corrected by using");
    printf(" the \n and \\ escape sequences");
    return 0;
}
```

Can you see where the format issues are? What's missing, and where should the correction or corrections be placed? The next block of code—and its output in Figure 1.12—corrects the format issues with appropriately placed escape sequences.

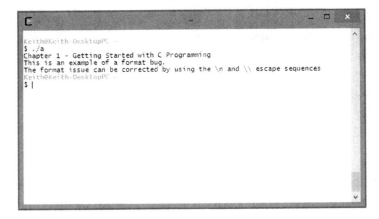

Figure 1.12
Correcting the format bugs by adding \n and \\ escape sequences where needed.

```c
#include <stdio.h>

int main()
{
    printf("Chapter 1 - Getting Started with C Programming\n");
    printf("This is an example of a format bug.\n");
    printf("The format issue can be corrected by using");
    printf(" the \\n and \\\\ escape sequences");
    return 0;
}
```

Format issues are common in beginning programming. Typically, you can resolve them quickly by practicing the printf() function and the various escape sequences.

Another common bug type is a logic error, including a loop that doesn't exit when expected, an incorrect mathematical equation, or perhaps a flawed test for equality (condition). The first step in debugging a logic error is to find the first line where the program bug exists. One way of doing this is through print statements, using the printf() function, scattered through your code. For example, you might do something like this in your source code:

```c
anyFunction(int x, int y)
{
    printf("Entering anyFunction()\n"); fflush(stdout);
    — lots of your code here ——
    printf("Exiting anyFunction()\n"); fflush(stdout);
}
```

The fflush() function ensures that the result of the printf statement is sent to your screen immediately, and you should use it if you're using printf()'s for debugging purposes. The stdout parameter passed to the fflush() function is the standard output, generally the computer screen.

After you have narrowed down the line or function where your logic error occurs, the next step is to find out the value of your variables at that time. You can also use the printf() function to print variable values, which aids you greatly in determining the source of abnormal program behavior. Displaying variable values using the printf() function is discussed in detail in Chapter 2, "Primary Data Types."

Remember, after you fix any bug, you must recompile your program, run it, and debug it again if necessary.

As a beginning programmer you will, more often than not, encounter compile errors rather than logic errors, which are generally the result of syntax issues such as missing identifiers and terminators or invalid directives, escape sequences, and comment blocks.

Debugging compile errors can be daunting, especially when you see 50 or more errors on the computer screen. One important thing to remember is that a single error at the top of your program can cause cascading errors during compile time. Therefore, the best place to start debugging compile errors is with the first error on the list! In the next few sections, you'll explore some of the more common compile errors that beginning C programmers experience.

Common Error #1: Missing Program Block Identifiers

If you forget to insert a beginning or a corresponding ending program block identifier ({ or }), you will see error messages similar to those in Figure 1.13. In the example that follows, I have intentionally neglected to use the beginning program block identifier ({) after the main() function name.

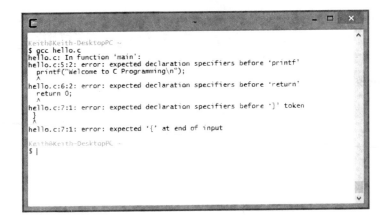

Figure 1.13
Errors caused by a missing program block identifier.

```
#include <stdio.h>

int main()
    printf("Welcome to C Programming\n");
return 0;
}
```

Yikes! Figure 1.13 shows lot of errors for simply forgetting to use the beginning program block identifier ({). When debugging compile errors, remember to start with the first error, shown next, which tells you there's an error right before the printf() function. You will find that solving the first error corrects many or all of the remaining errors.

```
hello.c:5:2: error: expected declaration specifiers before 'printf'
  printf("Welcome to C Programming\n");
  ^
```

Trick

To help you find the location of an error, the compiler attempts to show you the line number where an error is caught. In the preceding example, hello.c:5: is telling you that the error was caught five lines down in hello.c source code. Note that the compiler counts blank lines as well as lines with code when making this calculation for you.

Although the compiler error points to the beginning of printf, it's important to know that the problem is *not* with printf but with something preceding it—in this case, the missing block identifier.

Common Error #2: Missing Statement Terminators

Figure 1.13 depicts a common error message generated by a few common scenarios. This type of parse error can be generated for a couple of reasons. In addition to missing program block identifiers, parse errors can occur because of missing statement terminators (semicolons).

Figure 1.14 depicts a bug in the following program. Can you see where the bug is hiding?

```c
#include <stdio.h>

int main()
{
    printf("Welcome to C Programming\n")
    return 0;
}
```

Parse errors occur because the C compiler is unable to determine the end of a program statement such as a print statement. In the example shown in Figure 1.14, the C compiler (gcc) tells you that it expected a semicolon (statement terminator) on line 6 before the return statement.

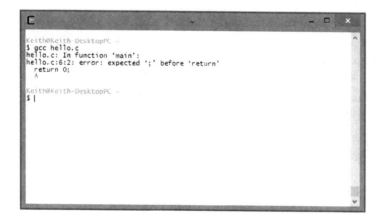

Figure 1.14
Error caused by a missing terminator.

Common Error #3: Invalid Preprocessor Directives

If you type an invalid preprocessor directive, such as misspelling a library name, you receive an error message similar to Figure 1.15.

The following program block with a misspelled library name in the preprocessor directive caused the error generated in Figure 1.15. Can you see the error?

```c
#include <sdio.h>

int main()
{
    printf("Welcome to C Programming\n");
    return 0;
}
```

This error was caused because the library file `sdio.h` does not exist. You should spell the library name for standard input output as `stdio.h`.

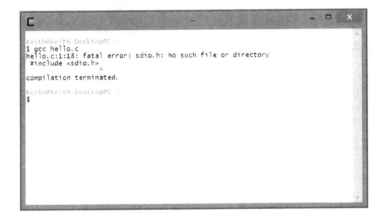

Figure 1.15
Error caused by invalid preprocessor directive.

Common Error #4: Invalid Escape Sequences

When using escape sequences, it is common to employ invalid characters or invalid character sequences. For example, Figure 1.16 depicts an error generated by an invalid escape sequence.

As shown in Figure 1.16, the gcc compiler is more specific about this error. Specifically, it notes that the error is on line 7 and that it is an unknown escape sequence.

Figure 1.16 Error caused by invalid escape sequence.

Can you identify the invalid escape sequence in the following program?

```c
#include <stdio.h>

int main()
{
    printf("Welcome to C Programming\m");
return 0;
}
```

Replacing the invalid escape sequence \m with a valid sequence such as \n corrects the problem.

Common Error #5: Invalid Comment Blocks

As mentioned earlier in the "Using Comments" section of this chapter, invalid comment blocks can generate compile errors, as shown in Figure 1.17.

```c
#include <stdio.h>

int main()
{
    */ This demonstrates a common error with comment blocks /*
    printf("Welcome to C Programming\n");
    return 0;
}
```

A simple correction to the comment block, shown next, solves the issue and allows the program to compile successfully.

```c
/* This corrects the previous comment block error
```

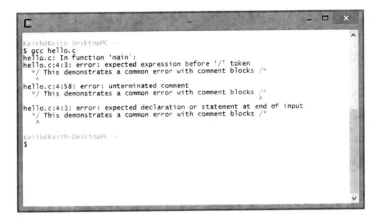

Figure 1.17
Errors generated by invalid comment blocks.

Summary

- Functions enable you to group a logical series of activities, or program statements, under one name.
- Functions can take in and pass back information.
- An algorithm is a finite step-by-step process for solving a problem.
- Each function implementation requires that you use a beginning brace ({) and a closing brace (}).
- Comments help to identify program purpose and explain complex routines.
- The character set /* signifies the beginning of a comment block, and the character set */ identifies the end of a comment block.
- Thirty-two words are defined as keywords in the standard ANSI C programming language; these keywords have predefined uses and cannot be used for any other purpose in a C program.
- Most program statements control program execution and functionality and may require a program statement terminator (;).
- Program statements that do not require a terminator include preprocessor directives, comment blocks, and function headers.
- The printf() function is used to display output to the computer screen.
- When combined with the backslash (\), special characters such as n make up an escape sequence.
- The library name stdio.h is short for standard input output and contains links to various standard C library functions, such as printf().

- C compilers such as gcc preprocess program code, generate error codes and messages if applicable, compile program code into object code, and link any necessary libraries.
- Compile errors are generally the result of syntax issues, including missing identifiers and terminators, or invalid directives, escape sequences, and comment blocks.
- A single error at the top of your program can cause cascading errors during compile time.
- The best place to start debugging compile errors is with the first error.

Challenges

1. Study the Vim Quick Guide in Appendix B.
2. Study the nano Quick Guide in Appendix C.
3. Study the Tiny C Compiler (TCC) Quick Guide in Appendix D.
4. Create a program that prints your name.
5. Create a program that uses escape sequence \" to print your favorite quote.
6. Create a program that uses escape sequence \\ to print the following directory structure: c:\cygwin\home\administrator.
7. Write a program that prints a diamond, as shown here:

```
        *
     *     *
   *           *
  *             *
   *           *
     *     *
        *
```

8. Create a calendar program using the current month (similar to the one shown in Figure 1.6).

2

Primary Data Types

This chapter teaches you essential computer memory concepts, as well as how to get information from users and store it as data using C language data types. You learn how to display variable contents using the `printf()` function and how to manipulate data stored in variables using basic arithmetic. Specifically, this chapter covers the following topics:

- Exploring memory concepts
- Understanding data types
- Initializing variables and the assignment operator
- Printing variable contents
- Using conversion specifiers
- Understanding constants
- Using programmatic conventions and styles
- Doing arithmetic in C
- Understanding operator precedence
- Chapter program: Shop Profit

Exploring Memory Concepts

A computer's memory is somewhat like a human's, in that a computer has both short-term and long-term memory. A computer's long-term memory is called *nonvolatile* memory and is generally associated with mass storage devices, such as hard drives, large disk arrays, optical storage (CD/DVD), and of course portable storage devices such as Universal Serial Bus (USB) flash or thumb drives. In Chapter 10, "Dynamic Memory Allocation," and Chapter 11, "File Input and Output," you learn how to use nonvolatile memory for storing data.

This chapter's focus is on a computer's short-term, or *volatile,* memory. Volatile memory loses its data when power is removed from the computer. Volatile memory is commonly referred to as RAM (Random Access Memory).

RAM is composed of fixed-size cells, with each cell number referenced through an address. Programmers commonly reference memory cells through the use of variables. There are many types of variables, depending on the programming language, but all variables share similar characteristics, as described in Table 2.1.

TABLE 2.1 COMMON VARIABLE CHARACTERISTICS

Attribute	Description
Name	The name of the variable used to reference data in program code
Type	The data type of the variable (number, character, and so on)
Value	The data value assigned to the variable's memory location
Address	The address assigned to a variable, which points to a memory cell location

Using the attributes defined in Table 2.1, Table 2.2 depicts the relationship for some common data types. Note that the letters and numbers in the "Memory Address" column in Table 2.2, such as BA40, represent example memory locations in the hexadecimal numbering system. Because it is easier to represent binary numbers in the hexadecimal numbering system than in the decimal numbering system, hexadecimal notation is used in advanced C programming to reference memory addresses.

TABLE 2.2 COMMON VARIABLE ATTRIBUTES AND SAMPLE VALUES

Variable Name	Value	Type	Memory Address
operand1	29	integer	BA40
result	756.21	float	1AD0
initial	M	char	8C70

Understanding Data Types

You will work with many types of data in your programming career, such as numbers, dates, strings, Booleans, arrays, objects, and data structures. Each type of data is categorized in C as a specific data type, and this data type is, unsurprisingly, a data storage format that can contain a specific type or range of values. Although this book covers some of the aforementioned data types in later chapters, this chapter concentrates on the following primary data types:

- Integers
- Floating-point numbers
- Characters

Using Integers

Integers are whole numbers that represent positive and negative numbers, such as –3, –2, –1, 0, 1, 2, and 3, but not fractional numbers or numbers with a decimal place.

Integer data types hold a maximum of four bytes of information and are declared with the int (short for integer) keyword, as shown in the following line of code:

```
int x;
```

In C, you can declare more than one variable on the same line using a single int declaration statement, with each variable name separated by commas, as demonstrated here:

```
int x, y, z;
```

The preceding variable declaration declares three integer variables named x, y, and z. Remember from Chapter 1, "Getting Started with C Programming," that executable program statements such as a print statement, or in this case a variable declaration, require a statement terminator (;).

> **Hint**
>
> *Floating-point numbers* are very large and very small positive and negative numbers with decimals to indicate different degrees of accuracy, depending on your needs. For example, in a program used to guide an airplane's altitude, being precise to 0.001 meters (a millimeter) would be overkill, but in a program used to guide a microchip creation, a difference of 0.001 meters is huge.

Signed numbers include positive and negative numbers, whereas unsigned numbers can only include positive values. Here are some examples of floating-point numbers:

- 09.4543
- 3428.27
- 112.34329
- −342.66
- −55433.33281

Use the keyword `float` to declare floating-point numbers, as shown next:

```
float operand1;
float operand2;
float result;
```

The preceding code declares three floating-point variable data types called operand1, operand2, and result.

Using Characters

Character data types are representations of integer values known as *character codes*. For example, the character code 90 represents the uppercase letter Z. Note that a lowercase z has a different character code (122).

Characters represent more than just the letters of the alphabet; they also represent numbers 0 through 9, special characters such as the asterisk (*) or even a blank space, and keyboard keys such as Del (delete) and Esc (escape). In all, there are a total of 128 common character codes (0 through 127) that make up the most commonly used characters of a keyboard.

Character codes are most notably organized through the American Standard Code for Information Interchange (ASCII) character set. For a listing of common ASCII character codes, see Appendix E, "ASCII Character Codes."

Hint

ASCII is noted for its character set, which uses small integer values to represent character or keyboard values.

In C, you create character variables using the char (short for character) keyword, as demonstrated here:

```
char firstInitial;
char middleInitial;
char lastInitial;
```

You must enclose character data assigned to character variables in single quotes ('), also known as tick marks or apostrophes. As you'll see in the next section, the equal sign (=) is used for assigning data to the character variable.

Trap

You cannot assign multiple characters to a single character variable type. When more than one character is needed for storing a single variable, you must use a character array (discussed in Chapter 6, "Arrays") or strings (discussed in Chapter 8, "Strings").

Initializing Variables and the Assignment Operator

When you first declare variables, the program assigns the variable name (address pointer) to an available memory location. It is never safe to assume that the newly assigned variable location is empty. It's possible that the memory location contains previously used data (or random garbage). To prevent unwanted data from appearing in your newly created variables, initialize the new variables, as shown in the following code snippet:

```
/* Declare variables */
int x;
char firstInitial;
/* Initialize variables */
x = 0;
firstInitial = '\0';
```

The preceding code declares two variables: x, which is an integer data type, and firstIntial, which is a character data type. After creating, or *declaring*, the two variables, I assign a particular initial value to them, a process known as *initialization*. For the integer variable, I assign the value zero (0), and for the character data type, I assign the character set \0, which is known as the NULL character.

Note that you must enclose the NULL character assignment, as with all character data assignments, in single quotes.

The NULL data type is commonly used to initialize memory locations in programming languages, such as C, and relational databases, such as Oracle and SQL Server.

Although NULL data types are a common computer science concept, they can be confusing. Essentially, NULL characters are unknown data types stored in a memory location. However, it is not proper to think of NULL data as empty or void; instead, think of NULL data as simply undefined.

It's a bit of a fine point, but when you initialize a variable with a value, the equal sign is not used as a *comparison* operator, but rather as an *assignment* operator. In other words, you would not say that x is equal to 0. Rather, you would say that the value 0 is being assigned to the variable x.

You can also initialize your variables while declaring them, as shown next:

```
int x = 0;
char firstInitial = '\0';
```

The preceding code accomplishes the same tasks in two lines as what the following code accomplishes in four:

```
int x;
char firstInitial;
x = 0;
firstInitial = '\0';
```

Printing Variable Contents

To print the contents of variables, use the printf() function with a few new formatting options, as demonstrated in the following code block:

```
#include <stdio.h>

int main()
{
    //variable declarations
    int x;
    float y;
    char c;
```

```
    //variable initializations
    x = -4443;
    y = 554.21;
    c = 'M';

    //printing variable contents to standard output
    printf("\nThe value of integer variable x is %d", x);
    printf("\nThe value of float variable y is %f", y);
    printf("\nThe value of character variable c is %c\n", c);
    return 0;
}
```

First, I declare three variables (one integer, one float, and one character), and then I initialize each of them. After initializing the variables, I use the printf() function and conversion specifiers (discussed next) to output each variable's contents to the computer screen.

The preceding code is a complete C program that demonstrates many of the topics discussed in this chapter thus far, and its output is shown in Figure 2.1.

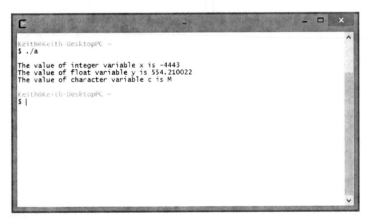

Figure 2.1
Printing variable contents.

Using Conversion Specifiers

Because information is stored as binary data in the computer's memory, and a series of 1s and 0s aren't especially fun to read, as a programmer in C, you must specifically tell input or output functions, such as printf(), how to display the data as information in a more human-friendly format. You can accomplish this seemingly difficult task using character sets known as *conversion specifiers*.

Conversion specifiers are composed of two characters: The first character is the percent sign (%), and the second is a special character that tells the program how to convert the data. Table 2.3 describes the most common conversion specifiers for the data types discussed in this chapter.

TABLE 2.3 COMMON CONVERSION SPECIFIERS USED WITH PRINTF()

Conversion Specifier	Description
%d	Displays signed integer value
%f	Displays signed floating-point value
%c	Displays single character value

Displaying Integer Data Types with printf()

Integer data types are displayed using the %d conversion specifier with a printf() statement:

```
printf("%d", 55);
```

The output of the preceding statement prints the following text:

55

You can also use the %d conversion specifier to display the contents of a variable declared as an integer data type, as demonstrated next.

```
int operand1;
operand1 = 29;
printf("The value of operand1 is %d", operand1);
```

In the preceding statements, I declare a new integer variable called operand1. Next, I assign the number 29 to the newly created variable and display its contents using the printf() function with the %d conversion specifier.

Each variable displayed using a printf() function must be inside the parentheses and separated with a comma (,).

Displaying Floating-Point Data Types with printf()

To display floating-point numbers, use the %f conversion specifier demonstrated next.

```
printf("%f", 55.55);
```

Here's another example of the %f conversion specifier, which prints the contents of a floating-point variable:

```
float result;
result = 3.123456;
printf("The value of result is %f", result);
```

Although the %f conversion specifier displays floating-point numbers, it may not be enough to display the floating-point number with correct or wanted precision. The following printf() function demonstrates the precision problem:

```
printf("%f", 55.55);
```

This printf() example outputs a floating-point number with a six-digit precision to the right of the decimal point, as shown next:

```
55.550000
```

To create precision with floating-point numbers, adjust the conversion specifier using numbering schemes between the % sign and the f character conversion specifier:

```
printf("%.1f", 3.123456);
printf("\n%.2f", 3.123456);
printf("\n%.3f", 3.123456);
printf("\n%.4f", 3.123456);
printf("\n%.5f", 3.123456);
printf("\n%.6f", 3.123456);
```

The preceding code block produces the following output:

```
3.1
3.12
3.123
3.1234
3.12345
3.123456
```

Notice that I've included the escape sequence \n in each of the preceding print statements (except the first line of code). Without the new line (\n) escape sequence, each statement's output generates on the same line, making it difficult to read.

Displaying Character Data Types with printf()

Characters are also easy to display using the %c conversion specifier:

```
printf("%c", 'M');
```

The output of this statement is simply the single letter M. Like the other conversion specifiers, you can output the contents of a character variable data type using the %c conversion specifier and a printf() function, as demonstrated next:

```
char firstInitial;
firstInitial = 'S';
printf("The value of firstInitial is %c", firstInitial);
```

You can use multiple conversion specifiers in a single printf() function:

```
char firstInitial, middleInitial, lastInitial;
firstInitial = 'M';
middleInitial = 'A';
lastInitial = 'V';
printf("My Initials are %c.%c.%c.", firstInitial, middleInitial, lastInitial);
```

The output of the preceding program statements is as follows:

```
My Initials are M.A.V.
```

Notice in the next statement that each variable displayed with the printf() function is outside the double quotes and separated with a single comma:

```
printf("My Initials are %c.%c.%c.", firstInitial, middleInitial, lastInitial);
```

Text inside of printf()'s double quotes is reserved for displayable text, conversion specifiers, and escape sequences.

Understanding Constants

Often referred to as read-only variables, constant data types cannot lose their data values during program execution. They are most commonly used when you need to reuse a common data value without changing it.

Constant data values can be of many data types but must be assigned when the constant is first created, as demonstrated next:

```
const int x = 20;
const float PI = 3.14;
```

Notice that the keyword const precedes the data-type name, signaling that this is a read-only variable or constant. You can print the values of constants in the same way that normal variables are printed using conversion specifiers with the printf() function, as shown in the following program code:

```
#include <stdio.h>

int main()
{
    const int x = 20;
    const float PI = 3.14;
    printf("\nConstant values are %d and %.2f\n", x, PI);
    return 0;
}
```

Figure 2.2 demonstrates the output of the preceding code block.

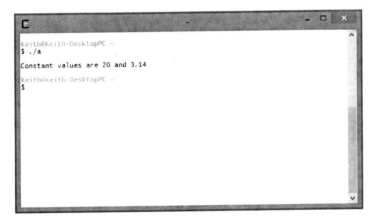

Figure 2.2
Printing constant data-type values.

Using Programming Conventions and Styles

Your programs are a reflection of you, and the source code should reveal a smooth and consistent style that guides the reader's eyes through algorithms and program flow. Just as a bridge provides function, it can also be aesthetically pleasing for both the structural engineer and the traveler.

You should stick with a style and convention that enable you or someone else to read your code easily. Once you pick or become comfortable with a programming style, the name of the game is consistency. In other words, stick with it; don't intermix naming conventions for variables or intermingle indenting styles within the same program.

When learning how to program, you should specifically consider at least two areas to develop a consistent programming convention and style:

- White space
- Variable naming conventions

Using White Space

White space is not often discussed in programming circles because it provides no computing benefits. In fact, the compiler ignores white space, so you're free to treat it as you may. What exactly is white space? Metaphorically speaking, white space is your programming canvas. Misused, it can strain the reader's eyes; painted properly, it can be a benefit. A couple examples of how white space can be controlled are with braces and indentation.

Indentation is a must because it guides your eyes in and out of program control. For example, looking at the following sample `main()` function, your eyes quickly tell you that the code inside the function logically belongs to it:

```
int main()
{
    //your code in here
}
```

A common discussion around indentation is the age-old argument of tabs versus spaces. This argument can be settled pretty easily in favor of spaces. The rationale behind this favor is based on the fact that tabs can be set to take up various columns. Another programmer opening your code might not have the same number of columns set for her tabs; consequently, the formatting will be off.

Another common question with beginning programmers is how far to indent. I prefer an indentation of two to four spaces. An indentation of longer than four spaces will eventually lead to lines that are too long. The goal here is to maintain a consistent indentation style that keeps the lines of code on the computer screen.

One more thing to consider regarding white space is your brace styles, which are closely tied to your indentation style. Just as with indentation, there are a number of brace styles, though you will likely favor either this one

```
int main()
{
//your code in here
}
```

or this one

```
int main(){
    //your code in here
}
```

As with any style, the choice is yours, but I recommend balancing a style both comfortable to you and consistent with what others on your team are using. In this book, I've used four spaces for each level of indentation.

Understanding Variable Naming Conventions

The following list contains a minimal number of guidelines you should follow when declaring and naming your variables:

- Identify data types with a prefix.
- Use uppercase and lowercase letters appropriately.
- Give variables meaningful names.

There is no one correct way of implementing a nomenclature for your variable names, although some are better than others. After identifying your naming standards, the most important process is to stay consistent with those practices throughout each of your programs.

In the next few sections, I show you a couple of different ways that have worked for me and for many other programmers who have used the guidelines in the preceding list.

Trap

In addition to adhering to a variable naming convention, be cautious not to use reserved characters in your variable names. As a general rule, abide by the following suggestions:

- Always begin your variable names with a lowercase letter.
- Do not use spaces in your variable names.
- Only use letters, numbers, and underscores (_) in your variable names.
- Keep variable names fewer than 31 characters to maintain American National Standards Institute (ANSI) C standards.

Identifying Data Types with a Prefix

When working with variables, I tend to choose one of three types of prefixes, as demonstrated next:

```
int intOperand1;
float fltResult;
char chrMiddleInitial;
```

For each variable data type, I choose a three-character prefix—int (short for integer), flt (short for float), or chr (short for character). When I see these variables in my program code, I know instantly what data types they are.

Another way of prefixing your integer data types is to use a single-character prefix, as shown in the second variable declarations:

```
int iOperand1;
float fResult;
char cMiddleInitial;
```

Even though these variables don't scream out their data types, you can see their prefix easily when trying to determine variable content type. Also, these single-character prefixes work well when used in conjunction with appropriate upper- and lowercase letters, as discussed in the next section.

Using Uppercase and Lowercase Letters Appropriately

Capitalizing the first character of each word in a variable name (as shown in the following code) is the most common and preferred variable naming convention:

```
float fNetSalary;
char cMenuSelection;
int iBikeInventoryTotal;
```

Using uppercase characters in each word makes it easy to read the variable name and identify its purpose. Now, take a look at the same variables with the same name, only this time without using uppercase characters:

```
float fnetsalary;
char cmenuselection;
int ibikeinventorytotal;
```

Which variable names are easier to read?

In addition to using uppercase letters for readability, some programmers like to use the underscore character to break up words, as shown in the following code:

```
float f_Net_Salary;
char c_Menu_Selection;
int i_Bike_Inventory_Total;
```

Using the underscore character certainly creates a readable variable, but it is a bit too cumbersome for me.

Constant data types provide another challenge for creating a standard naming convention. I like the following naming conventions:

```
const int constWeeks = 52;
const int WEEKS = 52;
```

In the first constant declaration, I use the const prefix for identifying constWeeks as a constant. Notice, though, that I still capitalize the first letter in the constant name for readability purposes.

In the second declaration, I simply capitalize every letter in the constant name. This naming style really stands out.

Giving Variables Meaningful Names

Giving your variables meaningful names is probably the most important part of variable naming conventions. Doing so creates self-documenting code. Consider the following section of code, which uses comments to describe the variable's purpose:

```
int x; //x is the Age
int y; //y is the Distance
int z; //z is the Result
```

The preceding variable declarations do not use meaningful names and thus require some form of documentation to make your code's purpose understandable. Instead, look at the following self-documenting variable names.

```
int iAge;
int iDistance;
int iResult;
```

Using the scanf() Function

So far, you have learned how to send output to the computer's screen using the printf() function. In this section, you learn how to receive input from users through the scanf() function.

The scanf() function is another built-in function provided by the standard input output library <stdio.h>; it reads standard input from the keyboard and stores it in previously declared variables. It takes two arguments:

```
scanf("conversion specifier", variable);
```

The conversion specifier argument tells scanf() how to convert the incoming data. You can use the same conversion specifiers as discussed in Table 2.3 and shown again as relative to scanf() in Table 2.4.

TABLE 2.4 COMMON CONVERSION SPECIFIERS USED WITH SCANF()

Conversion Specifier	Description
%d	Receives integer value
%f	Receives floating-point number
%c	Receives character

The following code represents a complete C program, the Adder program, which uses the scanf() function to read in two integers and add them. Its output is shown in Figure 2.3.

```c
#include <stdio.h>

int main()
{
    int iOperand1 = 0;
    int iOperand2 = 0;
    printf("\n\tAdder Program, by Keith Davenport\n");
    printf("\nEnter first operand: ");
    scanf("%d", &iOperand1);
    printf("Enter second operand: ");
    scanf("%d", &iOperand2);
    printf("The result is %d\n", iOperand1 + iOperand2);
    return 0;
}
```

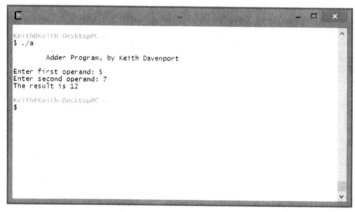

Figure 2.3
Using scanf() to receive input from a user.

The first notable line of code prompts the user to enter a number:

```c
printf("\nEnter first operand: ");
```

You may notice that the preceding printf() function neither contains a variable at the end nor includes the escape sequence \n at the end of the statement. When you leave the new line escape sequence off the end of the printf statement, program control pauses at the proper spot while waiting for user input.

The next line of code uses the `scanf()` function to receive input from the user:

```
scanf("%d", &iOperand1);
```

The first `scanf()` argument takes the integer conversion specifier (`"%d"`), which tells the program to convert the incoming value to an integer. The second operator is an address operator (&), followed by the name of the variable.

Essentially, the address operator contains a pointer to the location in memory where your variable is located. You will learn more about the address operator (&) in Chapter 7, "Pointers," when I discuss, unsurprisingly, pointers. For now, just know that you must precede variable names with the address operator when using the `scanf()` function.

Trap

Forgetting to place the address operator (&) in front of your variable in a `scanf()` function does not always generate compile errors, but it causes problems with memory access during program execution.

After receiving both numbers (operands) from the user, I then use a print statement to display the following result.

```
printf("The result is %d\n", iOperand1 + iOperand2);
```

In this print statement, I include a single conversion specifier (%d), which tells the program to display a single integer value. In the next argument of the `printf()` function, I add both numbers input by the user using the addition sign (+).

Doing Arithmetic in C

As demonstrated in the Adder program from the previous section, C enables programmers to perform all types of arithmetic. Table 2.5 demonstrates the most common arithmetic operators used in beginning C programming.

In the Adder program from the previous section, I used a shortcut when dealing with common arithmetic: I performed my calculation in the `printf()` function. Although it is not required, you can use additional variables and program statements to derive the same outcome. For example, the following code is another variation of the Adder program that uses additional program statements to achieve the same result.

TABLE 2.5 COMMON ARITHMETIC OPERATORS

Operator	Description	Example
*	Multiplication	fResult = fOperand1 * fOperand2;
/	Division	fResult = fOperand1 / fOperand2;
%	Modulus (remainder)	fRemainder = fOperand1 % fOperand2;
+	Addition	fResult = fOperand1 + fOperand2;
−	Subtraction	fResult = fOperand1 - fOperand2;

```c
#include <stdio.h>

int main()
{
    int iOperand1 = 0;
    int iOperand2 = 0;
    int iResult = 0;

    printf("\n\tAdder Program, by Keith Davenport\n");
    printf("\nEnter first operand: ");
    scanf("%d", &iOperand1);

    printf("Enter second operand: ");
    scanf("%d", &iOperand2);

    iResult = iOperand1 + iOperand2;
    printf("The result is %d\n", iResult);
    return 0;
}
```

In this version of the Adder program, I used two additional statements to derive the same outcome. Instead of performing the arithmetic in the printf() function, I've declared an additional variable called iResult and assigned to it the result of iOperand1 + iOperand2 using a separate statement, as demonstrated next.

```c
iResult = iOperand1 + iOperand2;
```

Remember that the equal sign (=) is an assignment operator, where the right side is being assigned to the left side of the operator (=). For example, you would not say the following:

    iResult equals iOperand1 plus iOperand2.

That is incorrectly stated. Instead, you would say:

    iResult gets the value of iOperand1 plus iOperand2.

Understanding Operator Precedence

Operator precedence is important when dealing with arithmetic in any programming language. Operator precedence in C is shown in Table 2.6.

TABLE 2.6 OPERATOR PRECEDENCE

Order or Precedence	Description
( )	Parentheses are evaluated first, from innermost to outermost
*, /, %	These are evaluated second, from left to right
+, −	These are evaluated last, from left to right

Take the following formula, for example, which uses parentheses to dictate the proper order of operations:

f = (a − b)(x − y);

Given a = 5, b = 1, x = 10, and y = 5, you could implement the formula in C using the following syntax:

intF = (5 − 1) * (10 − 5);

Using the correct order of operations, the value of intF would be 20. Take another look at the same implementation in C—this time without using parentheses to dictate the correct order of operations.

intF = 5 − 1 * 10 − 5;

Neglecting to implement the correct order of operations, intF would result in −10.

Chapter Program: Shop Profit

This chapter's simple program could be part of a calculation that a merchant shop in a game uses to sell gear to a player. As shown in Figure 2.4, the Shop Profit program uses many chapter-based concepts, such as variables, input and output with printf() and scanf() functions, and beginning arithmetic.

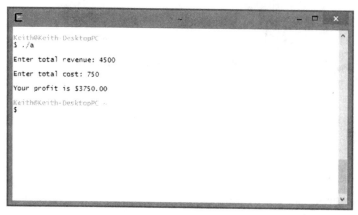

Figure 2.4
Demonstrating chapter-based concepts with the Shop Profit program.

All the C code needed to create the Shop Profit program is given here:

```c
#include <stdio.h>

int main()
{
    float fRevenue, fCost;
            /* profit = revenue - cost */

    printf("\nEnter total revenue: ");
    scanf("%f", &fRevenue);

    printf("\nEnter total cost: ");
    scanf("%f", &fCost);

    printf("\nYour profit is $%.2f\n", fRevenue - fCost);
    return 0;
}
```

Summary

- A computer's long-term memory is called nonvolatile memory and is generally associated with mass storage devices such as hard drives, large disk arrays, diskettes, and CD-ROMs.

- A computer's short-term memory is called volatile memory; it loses its data when power is removed from the computer.

- Integers are whole numbers that represent positive and negative numbers.

- Floating-point numbers represent all numbers, including signed and unsigned decimal and fractional numbers.

- Signed numbers include positive and negative numbers, whereas unsigned numbers can only include positive values.

- Character data types are representations of integer values known as character codes.

- Conversion specifiers are used to display unreadable data in a computer's memory as information.

- Constant data types retain their data values during program execution.

- White space is ignored by compilers and is commonly managed for readability using programming styles such as indentation and brace placement.

- Here are three useful rules for naming conventions:

    1. Identify data types with a prefix.

    2. Use upper- and lowercase letters appropriately.

    3. Give variables meaningful names.

- The scanf() function reads standard input from the keyboard and stores it in previously declared variables.

- The equal sign (=) is an assignment operator, where the right side of the assignment operator is assigned to the left side of the operator.

- In operator precedence, parentheses are evaluated first, from innermost to outermost.

1. Given a = 5, b = 1, x = 10, and y = 5, create a program that outputs the result of the formula f = (a − b)(x − y) using a single printf() function.

2. Create a program that uses the preceding formula and displays the result, but this time, prompt the user for the values a, b, x, and y. Use appropriate variable names and naming conventions.

3. Create a program that prompts a user for a character name. Store the user's chosen name using the scanf() function, and return a greeting to the character using that name.

4. Create a Shop Revenue program that, using the following formula, prompts a user for numbers to determine total revenue for a merchant selling gear:

   Total Revenue = Price * Quantity.

5. Build a Shop Commission program that prompts a user for data and determines the commission for a merchant selling gear using the following formula:

   Commission = Rate * (Sales Price − Cost).

3

Conditions

Conditions (often called program control, decisions, or expressions) enable you to create a program that performs different computational tasks or actions depending on whether a certain condition is true. Learning how to use and build conditions in your program code gives you a more fluid, interesting, and interactive program.

Along the way, I introduce essential beginning computer science theories that teach you the fundamental concepts of algorithm analysis and Boolean algebra. Reviewing these topics gives you the necessary background to understand conditional program control.

Specifically, this chapter covers the following topics:

- Algorithms for conditions
- Simple `if` structures
- Nested `if` structures
- Introduction to Boolean algebra
- Compound `if` structures and input validation
- The `switch` structure
- Random numbers
- Chapter program: Fortune Cookie

Algorithms for Conditions

Algorithms are the foundation for computer science. In fact, many computer science professors say that computer science is really the analysis of algorithms.

An *algorithm* is a finite step-by-step process for solving a problem that begins with a problem statement. As a programmer, you use this problem statement to formulate an algorithm for solving the problem. This process of building algorithms and algorithm analysis occurs before you write any program code.

To visualize algorithms, programmers and analysts commonly use one of two tools to demonstrate program flow (the algorithm). In the next few sections, I show you how to build and use two algorithm tools: pseudocode and flowcharts.

Expressions and Conditional Operators

Conditional operators are a key factor when building and evaluating expressions in pseudocode, flowcharts, or any programming language.

Not all programming languages, however, use the same conditional operators, so it is important to note what operators C uses.

Table 3.1 lists the conditional operators used in C.

TABLE 3.1 CONDITIONAL OPERATORS	
Operator	**Description**
==	Equal (two equal signs)
!=	Not equal
>	Greater than
<	Less than
>=	Greater than or equal to
<=	Less than or equal to

When you use conditional operators to build expressions (conditions), the result is either `true` or `false`. Table 3.2 demonstrates the `true`/`false` results when using conditional operators.

Pseudocode

Programmers frequently use *pseudocode* to aid in developing algorithms. It is primarily a marriage between human-like language and actual programming language. Because of pseudocode's likeness to programming syntax, it has always been more popular among programmers than analysts.

TABLE 3.2 EXPRESSIONS DEMONSTRATED	
Expression	Result
5 == 5	true
5 != 5	false
5 > 5	false
5 < 5	false
5 >= 5	true
5 <= 5	true

Because there are many different programming languages with varying syntax, pseudocode can easily vary from one programmer to another. For example, even though two programmers are solving the same problem, a C programmer's pseudocode may look a bit different from a Java programmer's pseudocode.

Nevertheless, if used appropriately and without heavy dependence on language specifics, pseudocode can be a wonderful and powerful tool for programmers to quickly write down and analyze an algorithm. Take the following problem statement, for example.

> Drink a health potion when a character's health is 100 or less. If health reaches 100 or more, resume battle.

Given this problem statement, my algorithm implemented in pseudocode looks like this:

```
if health <= 100
    Drink health potion
else
    Resume battle
end if
```

The preceding pseudocode uses a combination of language and programming syntax to depict the flow of the algorithm; however, if inserted into a C program, it would not compile. But creating usable code is not the point of pseudocode. Programmers use pseudocode as a shorthand notation for demonstrating what an algorithm looks like, but not necessarily for how the final program code appears. Once the pseudocode has been written down, you can easily transform it to any programming language.

How the pseudocode is written is ultimately up to you, but you should try to keep it as language independent as possible.

Here's another problem statement that requires the use of decision-making.

> Allow a character to deposit or withdraw gold from a game bank account, and if a user elects to withdraw gold, ensure that sufficient funds exist.

Pseudocode for this problem statement might look like the following:

```
if action == deposit
    Deposit gold into account
else
    if balance < amount requested
        Insufficient gold for transaction
    else
        Withdraw gold
    end if
end if
```

The first point of interest in the preceding pseudocode is that I have a nested condition inside a parent condition. This nested condition is said to belong to its parent condition, such that the nested condition is never evaluated unless one of the parent conditional requirements is met. In this case, the action must not equal the deposit for the nested condition to be evaluated.

Also notice that for each algorithm implemented with pseudocode, I use a standard form of indentation to improve the readability.

Take a look at the same pseudocode—this time without the use of indentation:

```
if action == deposit
Deposit gold into account
else
if balance < amount requested
Insufficient gold for transaction
else
Withdraw gold
end if
end if
```

You probably already see the benefit of using indentation for readability; the preceding pseudocode is difficult to read and follow. Without indentation in your pseudocode or actual program code, it is extremely difficult to pinpoint nested conditions.

In the next section, you learn how to implement the same algorithms, shown previously, with flowcharts.

Flowcharts

Popular among computing analysts, *flowcharts* use graphical symbols to depict an algorithm or program flow. In this section, I use four common flowchart symbols to depict program flow, as shown in Figure 3.1.

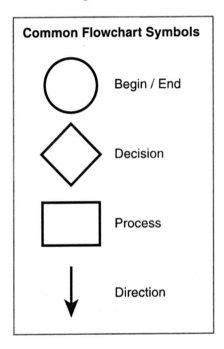

Figure 3.1
Common flowchart symbols.

To demonstrate flowchart techniques, take another look at the health potion algorithm used in the previous section:

```
if health <= 100
     Drink health potion
else
     Resume battle
end if
```

This health potion algorithm can also be easily represented using flowchart techniques, as shown in Figure 3.2.

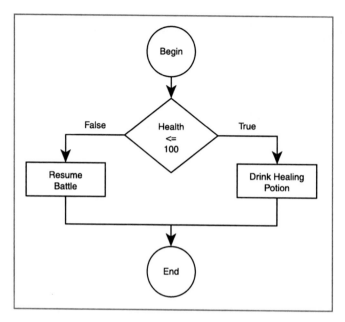

Figure 3.2
Flowchart for the health potion algorithm.

The flowchart in Figure 3.2 uses a decision symbol to illustrate an expression. If the expression evaluates to true, program flow moves to the right, processes a statement, and then terminates. If the expression evaluates to false, program flow moves to the left, processes a different statement, and then terminates.

As a general rule of thumb, your flowchart's decision symbols should always move to the right when an expression evaluates to true. However, sometimes you will not care if an expression evaluates to false. For example, take a look at the following algorithm implemented in pseudocode:

```
if target hit == true
    Increment player's score
end if
```

In the preceding pseudocode, I'm only concerned about incrementing the player's score when a target has been hit. I could demonstrate the same algorithm using a flowchart, as shown in Figure 3.3.

You can still use flowcharts to depict more complicated decisions, such as nested conditions, but you must pay closer attention to program flow. To demonstrate, take another look at the pseudocode used earlier to depict a sample banking process.

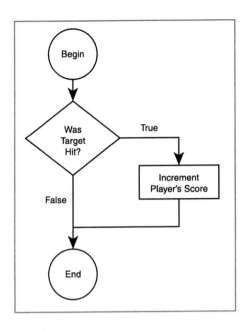

Figure 3.3
Flowchart for the target hit algorithm.

```
if action == deposit
    Deposit gold into account
else
    if balance < amount requested
        Insufficient gold for transaction
    else
        Withdraw gold
    end if
end if
```

The flowchart version of this algorithm is shown in Figure 3.4.

You can see in Figure 3.4 that I've used two diamond symbols to depict two separate decisions. But how do you know which diamond represents a nested condition? Good question. When looking at flowcharts, it can be difficult to see nested conditions at first, but remember that anything (process or condition) after the first diamond symbol (condition) actually belongs to that condition and therefore is nested inside it.

In the next few sections, I'll go from theory to application and discuss how to use C's if structure to implement simple, nested, and compound conditions.

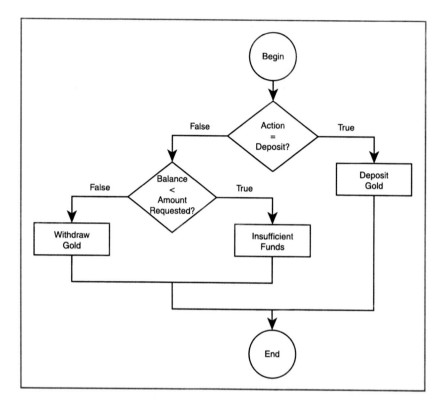

Figure 3.4
Flowchart for the
banking process.

Simple if Structures

As you will see shortly, the if structure in C is similar to the pseudocode discussed earlier, with a few minor exceptions. To demonstrate, take another look at the health potion algorithm in pseudocode form.

```
if health <= 100
     Drink health potion
else
     Resume battle
end if
```

The preceding pseudocode is implemented in C, as demonstrated next.

```
if (iHealth <= 100)
     //Drink health potion
else
     //Resume battle
```

The first statement is the condition, which checks for a `true` or `false` result in the expression (`iHealth <= 100`). You must enclose the expression in parentheses. If the expression's result is `true`, the `Drink health potion` code is executed; if the expression's result is `false`, the `else` part of the condition is executed. Also note that there is no end `if` statement in C.

If you process more than one statement inside your conditions, you must enclose the multiple statements in braces, as shown next:

```c
if (iHealth <= 100) {
    //Drink health potion
    printf("\nDrinking health potion!\n");
}
else {
    //Resume battle
    printf("\nResuming battle!\n");
}
```

The placement of each brace is only important in that braces begin and end the statement blocks. For example, I can change the placement of braces in the preceding code without affecting the outcome, as demonstrated next:

```c
if (IHealth <= 100)
{
    //Drink health potion
    printf("\nDrinking health potion!\n");
}
else
{
    //Resume battle
    printf("\nResuming battle!\n");
}
```

Consistency is the most important factor here. Simply choose a style of brace placement that works for you and stick with it.

Take a look at Figure 3.5, which is the output from a small program that uses basic `if` structures to implement these ideas.

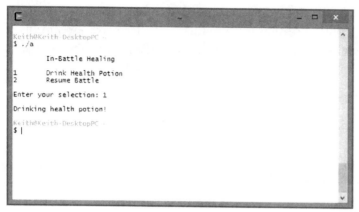

Figure 3.5
Demonstrating basic if structures.

The code needed to create the program illustrated in Figure 3.5 is shown here:

```c
#include <stdio.h>

int main()
{
    int iResponse = 0;

    printf("\n\tIn-Battle Healing\n");
    printf("\n1\tDrink Health Potion\n");
    printf("2\tResume Battle\n");

    printf("\nEnter your selection: ");
    scanf("%d", &iResponse);

    if (iResponse == 1)
        printf("\nDrinking health potion!\n");

    if (iResponse == 2)
        printf("\nResuming battle!\n");
    return 0;
}
```

First, I use the printf() functions to display a menu system. Next, I use the scanf() function to receive the user's selection and, finally, I compare the user's input (using if structures) against two separate valid numbers. Depending on the conditions' results, the program displays a message to the user.

Notice in my if structure that I'm comparing an integer variable to a number. This is acceptable—you can use variables in your if structures as long as you are comparing apples to apples and oranges to oranges. In other words, you can use a combination of variables and other data in your expressions as long as you're comparing numbers to numbers and characters to characters.

To demonstrate, here's the same program code again, this time using characters as menu choices:

```c
#include <stdio.h>

int main()
{
    char cResponse = '\0';

    printf("\n\tIn-Battle Healing\n");
    printf("\na\tDrink Health Potion\n");
    printf("b\tResume Battle\n");

    printf("\nEnter your selection: ");
    scanf("%c", &cResponse);

    if (cResponse == 'a')
        printf("\nDrinking health potion!\n");

    if (cResponse == 'b')
        printf("\nResuming battle!\n");
    return 0;
}
```

I changed my variable from an integer data type to a character data type and modified my scanf() function and if structures to accommodate the use of a character-based menu.

Nested if Structures

Take another look at the banking process implemented in pseudocode to demonstrate nested if structures in C:

```
if action == deposit
    Deposit gold into account
else
    if balance < amount requested
        Insufficient gold for transaction
```

```
    else
        Withdraw gold
    end if
end if
```

Because there are multiple statements inside the parent condition's else clause, I need to use braces when implementing the algorithm in C (shown next).

```c
if (action == deposit) {
    //deposit gold into account
    printf("\nGold deposited\n");
}
else {
    if (balance < amount_requested)
        //insufficient gold
    else
        //withdraw gold
}
```

For the purpose of this simple banking system, I hard-coded an initial balance into the variable declaration. You can see sample output from the banking system in Figure 3.6.

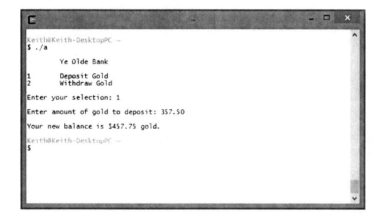

Figure 3.6
Demonstrating nested if structures with banking system rules.

```c
#include <stdio.h>

int main()
{
    int iSelection = 0;
    float fTransAmount = 0.0;
    float fBalance = 100.25;
```

```
    printf("\n\tYe Olde Bank\n");
    printf("\n1\tDeposit Gold\n");
    printf("2\tWithdraw Gold\n");

    printf("\nEnter your selection: ");
    scanf("%d", &iSelection);

    if (iSelection == 1) {
        printf("\nEnter amount of gold to deposit: ");
        scanf("%f", &fTransAmount);
        printf("\nYour new balance is: $%.2f gold\n", fBalance + fTransAmount);
    } //end if

    if (iSelection == 2) {
        printf("\nEnter amount of gold to withdraw: ");
        scanf("%f", &fTransAmount);
        if (fTransAmount > fBalance)
            printf("\nInsufficient funds\n");

        else
            printf("\nYour new balance is $%.2f gold\n", fBalance - fTransAmount);
    } //end if
    return 0;
} //end main function
```

Notice my use of comments when working with the if structures to denote the end of logical blocks. Essentially, I do this to minimize confusion about the purpose of many ending braces, which can litter even a simple program.

Introduction to Boolean Algebra

Before I discuss the next type of conditions, compound if structures, I want to give you some background on compound conditions using Boolean algebra.

As the subsequent sections discuss, Boolean algebra commonly uses three operators (and, or, and not) to manipulate two values (true and false).

BOOLEAN ALGEBRA

Boolean algebra is named after George Boole, a nineteenth-century English mathematician. Boole developed his own branch of mathematical logic that uses the values of true (denoted as a 1) and false (denoted as a 0). Boole's operations, unlike elementary algebra, were not based on addition and multiplication but rather on the operators and (conjunction), or (disjunction), and not (negation).

Even though Boole's work was before the advent of computers, his algebra is the foundation of modern digital electronics.

The and Operator

The and operator is used to build compound conditions. Each side of the condition must be true for the entire condition to be true. Take the following expression, for example:

3 == 3 and 4 == 4

This compound condition contains two separate expressions or conditions—one on each side of the and operator. The first condition evaluates to true, and so does the second condition, which generates a true result for the entire expression.

Here's another compound condition that evaluates to false:

3==4 and 4==4

This compound condition evaluates to false because one side of the and operator does not evaluate to true. Study Table 3.3 to get a better picture of possible outcomes with the and operator.

Truth tables enable you to see all possible scenarios in an expression containing compound conditions. The truth table in Table 3.3 shows two possible input values (x and y) for the and operator. As you can see, there is only one possible combination for the and operator to generate a true result: when both sides of the condition are true.

TABLE 3.3 TRUTH TABLE FOR THE AND OPERATOR

x	y	Result
true	true	true
true	false	false
false	true	false
false	false	false

The or Operator

The or operator is similar to the and operator in that it contains at least two separate expressions and is used to build a compound condition. The or operator, however, differs in that it only requires one side of the compound condition to be true for the entire expression to be true. Take the following compound condition, for example:

```
4 == 3 or 4 == 4
```

In the preceding compound condition, one side evaluates to false and the other to true, providing a true result for the entire expression. To demonstrate all possible scenarios for the or operator, study the truth table in Table 3.4.

TABLE 3.4 TRUTH TABLE FOR THE OR OPERATOR		
x	y	Result
true	true	true
true	false	true
false	true	true
false	false	false

Notice that Table 3.4 depicts only one scenario when the or operator generates a false outcome: when both sides of the operator result in false values.

The not Operator

The last Boolean operator I discuss in this chapter is the not operator. The not operator is easily understood at first but can certainly be a bit confusing when programmed in compound conditions.

Essentially, the not operator generates the opposite value of whatever the current result is. For example, the following expression uses the not operator in a compound condition:

```
not( 4 == 4 )
```

The inside expression, 4 == 4, evaluates to true, but the not operator forces the entire expression to result in false. In other words, the opposite of true is false.

Take a look at Table 3.5 to evaluate the not operator further.

TABLE 3.5 TRUTH TABLE FOR THE NOT OPERATOR	
x	**Result**
true	false
false	true

Notice that the not operator contains only one input variable (x) to build a compound condition.

Hint

C evaluates all nonzero values as true and all zero values as false.

Order of Operations

Now that you've seen how the Boolean operators and, or, and not work, you can further your problem-solving skills with Boolean algebra. Before you take that plunge, however, you must understand order of operations as it relates to program execution.

Order of operations becomes extremely important when dealing with compound conditions in Boolean algebra or with implementation in any programming language.

To dictate the order of operations, use parentheses to build clarification into your compound conditions. For example, given that x = 1, y = 2, and z = 3, study the following compound condition:

z < y and x > z or y < z

Without using parentheses to dictate the order of operations, you must assume that the order of operations for the compound condition flows from left to right. To see how this works, I've broken down the problem in the following example:

1. First, the expression z < y and x > z is executed, which results in false and false and in the overall result of false.

2. Next, the expression false or y < z is executed, which results in true or true and in the overall value of true.

But when I change the order of operations using parentheses, I get a different result, as shown next:

```
z < y and (x > z or y < z)
```

1. First, (x > z or y < z) is evaluated, which results in false or true and in the overall value of true.
2. Next, the expression z < y and true are evaluated, which results in false and true and in the final value of false.

You should now see the consequence of using or not using parentheses to guide the order of operations.

Building Compound Conditions with Boolean Operators

Using Boolean operators and the order of operations, you can easily build and solve Boolean algebra problems. Practicing this type of problem solving strengthens your analytic abilities, which will ultimately make you a stronger programmer when you incorporate compound conditions into your programs.

Try to solve the following Boolean algebra problems, given

```
x == 5, y == 3, and z == 4
```

1. x > 3 and z == 4
2. y >= 3 or z > 4
3. NOT(x == 4 or y < z)
4. (z == 5 or x > 3) and (y == z or x < 10)

Table 3.6 lists the answers for the preceding Boolean algebra problems.

TABLE 3.6 ANSWERS TO BOOLEAN ALGEBRA PROBLEMS

Question	Answer
1	true
2	true
3	false
4	true

Compound if Structures and Input Validation

You can use your newly acquired knowledge of compound conditions to build compound if conditions in C, or any other programming language for that matter.

As in Boolean algebra, compound if conditions in C commonly use the operators and and or, as demonstrated in Table 3.7.

TABLE 3.7 COMMON CHARACTER SETS USED TO IMPLEMENT COMPOUND CONDITIONS

Character Set	Boolean Operator
&&	and
||	or

As you will see in the next few sections, you can use these character sets in various expressions to build compound conditions in C.

The && Operator

The && operator implements the and Boolean operator and uses two ampersands to evaluate a Boolean expression from left to right. Both sides of the operator must evaluate to true before the entire expression becomes true.

The following two code blocks demonstrate C's && operator in use. The first block of code uses the and operator (&&) in a compound if condition, which results in a true expression:

```
if ( 3 > 1 && 5 < 10 )
    printf("The entire expression is true\n");
```

The next compound if condition results in false:

```
if ( 3 > 5 && 5 < 5 )
    printf("The entire expression is false\n");
```

The || Operator

The || character set (or Boolean operator) uses two pipe characters to form a compound condition, which is also evaluated from left to right. If either side of the condition is true, the whole expression results in true.

The following code block demonstrates a compound if condition using the || operator, which results in a true expression:

```
if ( 3 > 5 || 5 <= 5 )
    printf("The entire expression is true\n");
```

The next compound condition evaluates to false because neither side of the || operator evaluates to true.

```
if ( 3 > 5 || 6 < 5 )
    printf("The entire expression is false\n");
```

Trick

Consider using braces around a single statement in an if condition. For example, the following program code

```
if ( 3 > 5 || 6 < 5 )
    printf("The entire expression is false\n");
```

is the same as

```
if ( 3 > 5 || 6 < 5 ) {
    printf("The entire expression is false\n");
}
```

Delineating a single-line if condition statement with braces helps to ensure that all subsequent modifications to the if statement remain free of logic errors. Lots of logic errors creep into code when programmers begin to add additional statements to the single line if bodies but neglect to add the braces.

Checking for Upper- and Lowercase

You may remember from Chapter 2, "Primary Data Types," that characters are represented by American Standard Code for Information Interchange (ASCII) character sets. The lowercase letter a, for example, is represented by ASCII character code 97, and the uppercase letter A is represented by ASCII character code 65.

So what does this mean to you or me? Take the following C program, for example:

```
#include <stdio.h>

int main()
{
    char cResponse = '\0'; printf("Enter the letter A: ");
```

```
    scanf("%c", &cResponse);

    if ( cResponse == 'A' )
        printf("\nCorrect response\n");
    else
        printf("\nIncorrect response\n");
    return 0;
}
```

In the preceding program, what response would you get after entering the letter a? You may guess that you would receive Incorrect response. This is because the ASCII value for uppercase letter A is not the same as the ASCII value for lowercase letter a. (To see a listing of common ASCII characters, visit Appendix E, "ASCII Character Codes.")

To build user-friendly programs, you should use compound conditions to check for both upper- and lowercase letters, as shown in the following modified if condition:

```
if ( cResponse == 'A' || cResponse == 'a' )
```

To build a complete and working compound condition, you must have two separate and valid conditions on each side of the operator. A common mistake among beginning programmers is to build an invalid expression on one or more of the operator's sides. The following compound conditions are invalid:

```
if ( cResponse == 'A' || 'a' )
if ( cResponse == 'A' || == 'a' )
if ( cResponse || cResponse )
```

None of the expressions is complete on both sides; therefore, the expressions are incorrectly built. Take another look at the correct version of this compound condition, shown next:

```
if ( cResponse == 'A' || cResponse == 'a' )
```

Checking for a Range of Values

Checking for a range of values is a common way for programmers to perform input validation. You can use compound conditions and relational operators to check for value ranges, as shown in the following program:

```
#include <stdio.h>

int main()
{
    int iResponse = 0;
```

```
    printf("Enter a number from 1 to 10: ");
    scanf("%d", &iResponse);

    if ( iResponse < 1 || iResponse > 10 )
        printf("\nNumber not in range\n");
    else
        printf("\nThank you\n");
    return 0;
}
```

The main construct of this program is the compound if condition. This compound expression uses the || (or) operator to evaluate two separate conditions. If either of the conditions results in true, I know that the user has entered a number that is not between 1 and 10.

The isdigit() Function

The isdigit() function is part of the character-handling library <ctype.h> and is a wonderful tool for aiding you in validating user input. Specifically, you can use the isdigit() function to verify that the user has entered either digits or nondigit characters. Moreover, the isdigit() function returns true if its passed-in value evaluates to a digit, and false (0) if not.

As shown next, the isdigit() function takes one parameter:

isdigit(*x*)

If the parameter x is a digit, the isdigit() function returns a true value; otherwise, a 0 or false is sent back to the calling expression.

Remember to include the <ctype.h> library in your program when using the isdigit() function, as demonstrated next:

```
#include <stdio.h>
#include <ctype.h>

int main()
{
    char cResponse = '\0';

    printf("\nPlease enter a letter: ");
    scanf("%c", &cResponse);

    if ( isdigit(cResponse) == 0 )
        printf("\nThank you\n");
    else
```

```
        printf("\nYou did not enter a letter\n");
    return 0;
}
```

This program uses the isdigit() function to verify that the user has entered a letter or nondigit. If the user enters, for example, the letter a, isdigit() returns a 0 (false). But if the user enters the number 7, isdigit() returns a true value.

The preceding program uses a false result from the isdigit() function to determine nondigit data. Take a look at the next program, which uses isdigit() in a more conventional manner:

```
#include <stdio.h>
#include <ctype.h>

int main()
{
    char cResponse = '\0';

    printf("\nPlease enter a digit: ");
    scanf("%c", &cResponse);

    if isdigit(cResponse)
        printf("\nThank you\n");
    else
        printf("\nYou did not enter a digit\n");
    return 0;
}
```

Notice that I did not evaluate the isdigit() function to anything in the preceding if condition. This means I do not need to surround my expression in parentheses.

You can do this in any if condition as long as the expression or function returns a true or false (Boolean) value. In this case, isdigit() does return true or false, which is sufficient for the C if condition. For example, if the user enters a 7, which I pass to isdigit()—isdigit() returns a true value that satisfies the condition.

Take another look at the condition part of the preceding program to ensure that you grasp this concept:

```
if isdigit(cResponse)
    printf("\nThank you\n");
else
    printf("\nYou did not enter a digit\n");
```

The switch Structure

The switch structure is another common language block used to evaluate conditions. It is most commonly used when programmers want to evaluate a user's response to a specific set of choices, such as when a user selects an item from a menu. The following code snippet demonstrates how the switch structure is built:

```
switch (x) {
    case 1:
        //x Is 1
    case 2:
        //x Is 2
    case 3:
        //x Is 3
    case 4:
        //x Is 4
} //end switch
```

Note that the preceding switch structure requires the use of braces.

In this example, the variable x is evaluated in each case structure following the switch statement. But how many case statements must you use? It depends on how many possibilities your switch variable contains.

For example, the following program uses the switch structure to evaluate a user's response from a menu:

```
#include <stdio.h>

int main()
{
    int iResponse = 0;

    printf("\n1\tSports\n");
    printf("2\tGeography\n");
    printf("3\tMusic\n");
    printf("4\tWorld Events\n");
    printf("\nPlease select a category (1-4): ");
    scanf("%d", &iResponse);

    switch (iResponse) {
        case 1:
            printf("\nYou selected sports questions\n");
```

```
    case 2:
        printf("You selected geography questions\n");
    case 3:
        printf("You selected music questions\n");
    case 4:
        printf("You selected world event questions\n");
} //end switch
return 0;
} //end main function
```

Notice the output of the program when I select category 1, as shown in Figure 3.7.

What's wrong with this program's output? When I selected category 1, I should have only been given one response—not four. This bug occurred because after the appropriate case statement is matched to the switch variable, the switch structure continues processing each case statement thereafter.

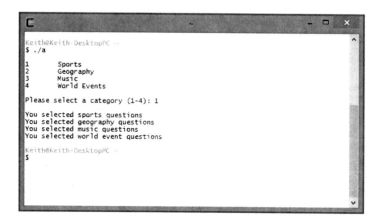

Figure 3.7
Demonstrating the switch structure.

You can solve this problem easily with the break keyword, as demonstrated next:

```
switch (iResponse) {
    case 1:
        printf("\nYou selected sports questions\n");
        break;
    case 2:
        printf("You selected geography questions\n");
        break;
    case 3:
        printf("You selected music questions\n");
        break;
    case 4:
```

```
        printf("You selected world event questions\n");
        break;
} //end switch
```

When C encounters a break statement inside a case block, it stops evaluating any further case statements.

The switch structure also comes with a default block, which you can use to catch any input that does not match the case statements. The following code block demonstrates the default switch section:

```
switch (iResponse) {
    case 1:
        printf("\nYou selected sports questions\n");
        break;
    case 2:
        printf("You selected geography questions\n");
        break;
    case 3:
        printf("You selected music questions\n");
        break;
    case 4:
        printf("You selected world event questions\n");
        break;
    default:
        printf("Invalid category\n");
} //end switch
```

In addition to evaluating numbers, the switch structure is popular when choosing between other characters, such as letters. Moreover, you can evaluate like data with multiple case structures on a single line, as shown next:

```
switch (cResponse) {
    case 'a': case 'A':
        printf("\nYou selected the character a or A\n");
        break;
    case 'b': case 'B':
        printf("You selected the character b or B\n");
        break;
    case 'c': case 'C'
        printf("You selected the character c or C\n");
        break;
} //end switch
```

Random Numbers

You can observe the concept and application of random numbers in all types of systems, from encryption programs to games. Fortunately for you and me, the C standard library offers built-in functions for generating random numbers. Most notable is the rand() function, which generates a whole number from 0 to a library-defined number, generally at least 32,767.

To generate a specific random set of numbers, say between 1 and 6 (the sides of a standard die, for example), you need to define a formula using the rand() function, as demonstrated next.

```
iRandom = (rand() % 6) + 1
```

Starting from the right side of the expression, I use the modulus operator (%) in conjunction with the integer 6 to generate seemingly random numbers between 0 and 5.

Remember that the rand() function generates random numbers starting with 0. To offset this fact, I simply add 1 to the outcome, which increments my random number range from 0 to 5 to 1 to 6. After a random number is generated, I assign it to the iRandom variable.

Here's another example of the rand() function implemented in a complete C program that prompts a user to guess a number from 1 to 10.

```c
#include <stdio.h>

int main()
{
    int iRandomNum = 0;
    int iResponse = 0;
    iRandomNum = (rand() % 10) + 1;

    printf("\nGuess a number between 1 and 10: ");
    scanf("%d", &iResponse);

    if (iResponse == iRandomNum)
        printf("\nYou guessed right\n");
    else {
        printf("\nSorry, you guessed wrong\n");
        printf("The correct guess was %d\n", iRandomNum);
    }
    return 0;
}
```

The only problem with this program, and the rand() function for that matter, is that the rand() function generates the same sequence of random numbers repeatedly. Unfortunately, after a user runs the program a few times, he begins to figure out that the numbers are not really random.

To correct this, use the srand() function, which produces a better pseudorandom number. More specifically, the srand() function tells the rand() function to produce a different random number every time it is executed.

> **Hint**
>
> **Why pseudorandom and not truly random? The numbers produced by the srand() function are not true random numbers because they are generated from a relatively small set of initial values. For most purposes, however, when executed properly, a time-seeded srand() function makes the number sequences generated by the rand() function sufficiently random.**

The srand() function takes an integer number as its starting point for randomizing. To give your program a better set of random numbers, pass the current time to the srand() function as shown next:

```
srand(time(NULL));
```

The time(NULL) function returns the current time in seconds, which is a perfect unpredictable integer number for the srand() function.

The srand() function only needs to be—and should only be—executed once in your program for it to perform randomization. In the preceding program, I would place the srand() function after my variable declarations but before the rand() function, as demonstrated in this snippet:

```
#include <stdio.h>

int main()
{
    int iRandomNum = 0;
    int iResponse = 0;
    srand(time(NULL));
    iRandomNum = (rand() % 10) + 1;
```

Chapter Program: Fortune Cookie

The Fortune Cookie program (shown in Figure 3.8) uses chapter-based concepts to build a small yet entertaining program that simulates an actual fortune found inside a fortune cookie. To build this program, I used the switch structure and random number generation.

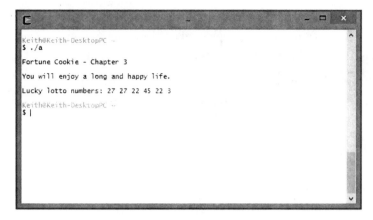

Figure 3.8
The Fortune Cookie program.

After reading this chapter and with some practice, you should be able to easily follow the Fortune Cookie program code and logic:

```c
#include <stdio.h>
#include <stdlib.h>
#include <time.h>

int main()
{
    int iRandomNum = 0;
    srand(time(NULL));
    iRandomNum = (rand() % 4) + 1;

    printf("\nFortune Cookie - Chapter 3\n");

    switch (iRandomNum) {
        case 1:
            printf("\nYou will meet a new friend today.\n");
            break;
        case 2:
            printf("\nYou will enjoy a long and happy life.\n");
            break;
        case 3:
            printf("\nOpportunity knocks softly. Can you hear it?\n");
            break;
        case 4:
            printf("\nYou'll be financially rewarded for your good deeds.\n");
```

```
            break;
    } //end switch

    printf("\nLucky lotto numbers: ");
    printf("%d ", (rand() % 49) + 1);
    printf("%d ", (rand() % 49) + 1);
    printf("%d ", (rand() % 49) + 1);
    printf("%d ", (rand() % 49) + 1);
    printf("%d ", (rand() % 49) + 1);
    printf("%d\n", (rand() % 49) + 1);
    return 0;
} //end main function
```

Summary

- When conditional operators are used to build expressions, the result is either true or false.
- Pseudocode is primarily a mix between human-like language and actual programming language and is frequently used by programmers to aid in developing algorithms.
- Flowcharts use graphical symbols to depict an algorithm or program flow.
- Conditions are implemented using the if structure, which contains an expression enclosed within parentheses.
- Boolean algebra commonly uses three operators (and, or, and not) to manipulate two values (true and false).
- Parentheses are used to dictate the order of operations and build clarification into compound conditions.
- You can use the isdigit() function to verify that the user has entered either digits or nondigit characters.
- The switch structure is used to evaluate conditions and is most commonly implemented when a specific set of choices requires evaluation.
- The rand() function generates a whole number from 0 to a library-defined number, generally at least 32,767.
- The srand() function tells the rand() function to produce a pseudorandom number every time it is executed.
- The time(NULL) function returns the current time in seconds, which is a good pseudorandom integer number for the srand() function.

1. Build a number-guessing game that uses input validation (isdigit() function) to verify that the user has entered a digit and not a nondigit (letter). Store a random number between 1 and 10 into a variable each time the program is run. Prompt the user to guess a number between 1 and 10 and alert the user if he was correct or not.

2. Build a Fortune Cookie program that uses either the Chinese Zodiac or astrological signs to generate a fortune, a prediction, or a horoscope based on the user's input. More specifically, the user may need to input her year of birth, month of birth, and day of birth depending on zodiac or astrological techniques used. With this information, generate a custom message or fortune. You can use the Internet to find more information on the Chinese Zodiac or astrology.

3. Create a dice game that uses two six-sided dice. Each time the program runs, use random numbers to assign values to each die variable. Output a "player wins" message to the user if the sum of the two dice is 7 or 11. Otherwise output the sum of the two dice and thank the user for playing.

4

Looping Structures

This chapter covers key programming constructs and techniques for building iteration into your C programs. An *iteration* is one execution of a section of program code, and *iterating* means repeating that code again and again until a specific condition is met. A *loop* is the actual sequence of program instructions that is repeated.

This chapter teaches you how looping structures use conditions to evaluate the number of times a loop should occur. Moreover, you learn the basic theory and design principals behind looping algorithms using pseudocode and flowcharting techniques. You also discover new techniques for assigning data and manipulating loops.

This chapter specifically covers the following:

- Pseudocode for loops
- Flowcharts for loops
- Additional operators
- The while loop
- The do while loop
- The for loop
- break and continue statements
- System calls
- Chapter program: Concentration

Pseudocode for Loops

Before I discuss the application of iteration, I'll show you some simple theory behind loops using basic algorithm techniques with pseudocode.

In Chapter 3, "Conditions," you learned that programmers express programming algorithms and key constructs using a combination of human-like language and programming syntax called pseudocode. As demonstrated in this section, you can also use pseudocode to express algorithms for looping structures.

Several situations require the use of looping techniques, also known as iteration. Here are some examples:

- Displaying a banking menu
- Playing a game until the player wins, loses, or quits
- Processing employee payroll data until the last employee is handled
- Calculating an amortization schedule for a loan
- Drinking a healing potion as long as a player's health is low
- Maintaining autopilot status until a flight crew turns it off

To demonstrate looping structures using pseudocode, I use processing employee payroll data as an example:

```
while end-of-file == false
    process employee payroll
loop
```

In this pseudocode, I first use a condition to evaluate whether the end of file has been read. If that condition is false (not end of file), I process employee data. In other words, I process the payroll until the end of file is true.

The condition in this loop may not be apparent at first, but it's similar to the conditions you learned in Chapter 3. The condition in the preceding example contains an expression that can only result in one of two values: true or false:

```
end-of-file == false
```

Notice a recurring theme between conditions and loops? The theme is simple: it's all about conditions! Both looping structures and conditions, such as the if condition and switch structure, use conditional expressions to evaluate whether something happens.

Now look at the following pseudocode example that loops through a theoretical payroll file to determine each employee's pay type (salary or hourly):

```
while end-of-file == false
    if pay-type == salary then
        pay = salary
    else
        pay = hours * rate
    end If
loop
```

Sometimes you want the loop's condition at the end, rather than at the beginning. To demonstrate, I can change the location of the loop's condition in the following pseudocode to ensure that a menu is displayed at least once to the end user:

```
do
    display menu
while user-selection != quit
```

By moving the condition to the bottom of the loop, I've guaranteed that the user has a chance to view the menu at least once.

Loops can contain all kinds of programming statements and structures, including nested conditions and loops. Nested loops provide an interesting study of algorithm analysis because they can be intensive in their process time.

The following block of pseudocode demonstrates the nested loop concept:

```
do
    display menu
    If user-selection == payroll then
        while end-of-file == false
            if pay-type == salary then
                pay = salary
            else
                pay = hours * rate
            end If
        loop
    end if
while user-selection != quit
```

In the preceding pseudocode, I first display a menu. If the user selects to process payroll, I enter a second or inner loop, which processes payroll until the end-of-file has been reached. Once the end-of-file has been reached, the outer loop's condition is evaluated to determine if the user wants to quit. If the user quits, program control is terminated; otherwise, the menu is displayed again.

Flowcharts for Loops

Using the same flowcharting symbols shown in Chapter 3, you can build flowcharts for loops.

To demonstrate loops in flowcharts, I use the pseudocode from the previous section, "Pseudocode for Loops." Specifically, I build a simple looping structure using a flowchart with the following pseudocode. The resulting flowchart is shown in Figure 4.1:

```
while end-of-file == false
      process employee payroll
loop
```

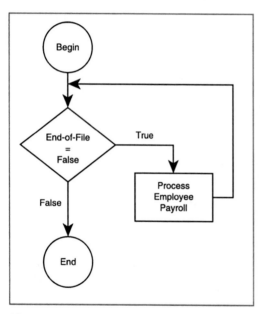

Figure 4.1
Flowchart demonstrating a simple looping structure.

In Figure 4.1, I use the diamond symbol to represent a loop. You might be wondering how to tell the difference between the diamond symbols that are used with conditions and loops in a flowchart. Figure 4.1 holds the answer. You can differentiate between conditions and loops in flowcharts by looking at the program flow. If you see connector lines that loop back to the beginning of a condition (diamond symbol), you know that the condition represents a loop. In this example, the program flow moves in a circular pattern. If the condition is true, employee payroll is processed and program control moves back to the beginning of the original condition. Only if the condition is false does the program flow terminate.

Take a look at the next set of pseudocode, which is implemented as a flowchart in Figure 4.2:

```
while end-of-file == false
    if pay-type == salary then
        pay = salary
    else
        pay = hours * rate
    end If
loop
```

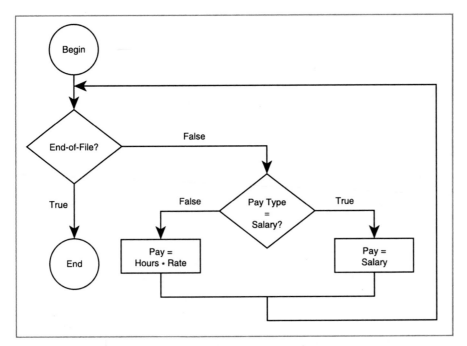

Figure 4.2
A flowchart that demonstrates a loop with an inner condition.

In Figure 4.2, you see that the first diamond symbol is really a loop's condition because program flow loops back to its beginning. Inside of the loop, however, is another diamond, which is not a loop. (The inner diamond does not contain program control that loops back to its origin.) Rather, the inner diamond's program flow moves back to the loop's condition regardless of its outcome.

Take another look at a previous pseudocode example (the flowchart is shown in Figure 4.3) that moves the condition to the end of the loop:

```
do
    display menu
while user-selection != quit
```

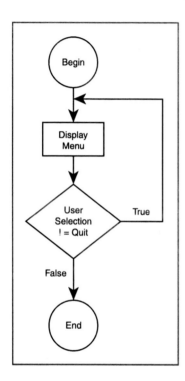

Figure 4.3
Moving a loop's condition to the end of the loop.

Remember that program flow is the key. Because the loop's condition in Figure 4.3 is at the end of the loop, the first process in the flowchart displays the menu. After displaying the menu, the loop's condition is encountered and evaluated. If the loop's condition is true, the program flow loops back to the first process; if it's false, the program flow terminates.

The final component to building looping algorithms with flowcharts is to demonstrate nested loops. Take another look at the nested loop pseudocode from the previous section:

```
do
    display menu
    If user-selection == payroll then
        while end-of-file != true
            if pay-type == salary then
```

```
            pay = salary
        else
            pay = hours * rate
        end If
    loop
  end if
while user-selection != quit
```

Figure 4.4 implements the preceding looping algorithm with flowcharting symbols and techniques.

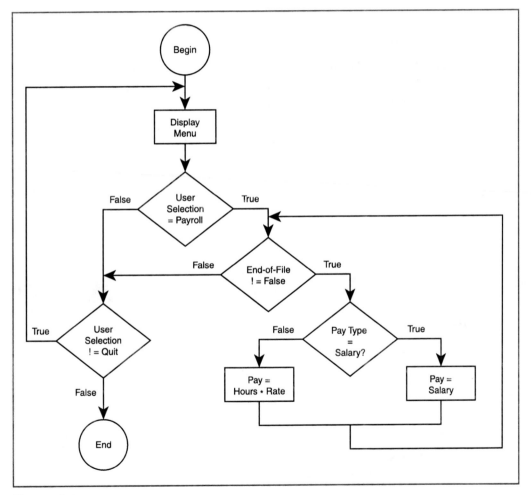

Figure 4.4
Using a flowchart to demonstrate nested loops.

Although Figure 4.4 is much more difficult to follow than the previous flowchart examples, you should still be able to identify the outer and inner (nested) loops by finding the diamonds that have program flow looping back their condition. Of the four diamonds in Figure 4.4, can you find the two that are loops? Again, to determine which diamond symbol represents a loop, simply identify each diamond that has program control returning to the top part of the diamond.

Here are the two loops in Figure 4.4 represented in pseudocode:

```
while end-of-file != false
while user-selection != quit
```

Additional Operators

You've already learned how to assign data to variables using the assignment operator (equal sign). In this section, I discuss operators for incrementing and decrementing number-based variables, and I introduce new operators for assigning data to variables.

> **Hint**
>
> To *increment* a variable is to increase its value by one. To *decrement* a variable is to decrease its value by one.

Table 4.1 shows the operators covered in the next four sections.

	TABLE 4.1 OPERATORS		
Operator	**Name**	**Syntax**	**Meaning**
++	Increment (postfix)	x++	Increment after expression is evaluated
	Increment (prefix)	++x	Increment before expression is evaluated
--	Decrement (postfix)	x--	Decrement after expression is evaluated
	Decrement (prefix)	--x	Decrement before expression is evaluated
+=	Addition Assignment	x+=y	x equals x plus y
-=	Subtraction Assignment	x-=y	x equals x minus y

Don't worry if the meanings are a little confusing. The idea that a variable can be incremented or decremented before or after an expression is evaluated can be a little strange until you see it in practice. The process will be clear once you've run the example code for each operator.

The ++ Operator

The **++** operator is useful for incrementing number-based variables by 1. To use the **++** operator, postfix it to (put it after) a variable, as shown next:

```
iNumberOfPlayers++;
```

To demonstrate further, study the following block of code, which uses the **++** operator to produce the output shown in Figure 4.5:

```c
#include <stdio.h>

int main()
{
    int x = 0;

    printf("\nThe value of x is %d\n", x);
    x++;
    printf("\nThe value of x is %d\n", x);
    return 0;
}
```

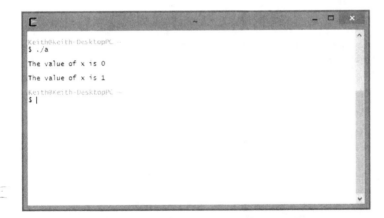

Figure 4.5
Incrementing number-based variables by 1 with the ++ operator.

You can use the increment operator (**++**) in two ways: As demonstrated earlier, you can postfix the increment operator to a variable, as shown:

```
x++;
```

This expression tells C to use the current value of variable x and increment it by 1. The variable's original value was 0 (that's what I initialized it to), and 1 was added to 0, which resulted in 1.

The other way to use the increment operator is to prefix it to (put it before) your variable, as demonstrated:

```
++x;
```

Changing the increment operator's placement (postfix versus prefix) with respect to the variable produces different results when evaluated. When the increment operator is placed to the left of the variable, it increments the variable's contents by 1 first, before it's used in another expression. To get a clearer picture of operator placement, study the following code, which generates the output shown in Figure 4.6:

```c
#include <stdio.h>

int main()
{
    int x = 0;
    int y = 0;

    printf("\nThe value of y is %d\n", y++);
    printf("\nThe value of x is %d\n", ++x);
    return 0;
}
```

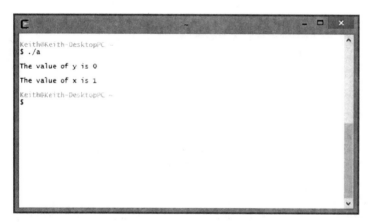

Figure 4.6
Demonstrating prefix and postfix increment operator placement in a sequential expression.

In the first `printf()` function, C prints the variable's value and then increments it. In the second `printf()` function, C increments the variable's value and then prints it.

This still may be a bit confusing, so study the following program, which further demonstrates increment operator placement:

```
#include <stdio.h>

int main()
{
    int x = 0;
    int y = 1;

    x = y++ * 2; //increments x after the assignment
    printf("\nThe value of x is: %d\n", x);

    x = 0;
    y = 1;
    x = ++y * 2; //increments x before the assignment
    printf("The value of x is: %d\n", x);
    return 0;
} //end main function
```

The preceding program produces the following output:

```
The value of x is: 2
The value of x is: 4
```

Even though most, if not all, C compilers run the preceding code the way you would expect, due to ANSI C compliance, the following statement can produce three different results with three different compilers:

anyFunction(++x, x, x++);

The argument ++x (using an increment prefix) is *not* guaranteed to be done before the other arguments (x and x++) are processed. In other words, there is no guarantee that each C compiler will process sequential expressions (an expression separated by commas) the same way.

Take a look at another example of postfix and prefix using the increment operator not in a sequential expression (C compiler neutral); the output is revealed in Figure 4.7.

```
#include <stdio.h>

int main()
{
    int x = 0;
    int y = 0;
```

```
    x = y++ * 4;
    printf("\nThe value of x is %d\n", x);

    y = 0; //reset variable value for demonstration purposes
    x = ++y * 4;
    printf("\nThe value of x is now %d\n", x);
    return 0;
}
```

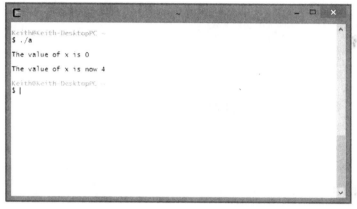

```
Keith@Keith-DesktopPC ~
$ ./a
The value of x is 0
The value of x is now 4
Keith@Keith-DesktopPC ~
$ |
```

Figure 4.7
Demonstrating prefix and postfix increment operator placement outside of a sequential expression (C compiler neutral).

The -- Operator

The -- operator is similar to the increment operator (++), but instead of incrementing number-based variables, it decrements them by 1. Also, like the increment operator, the decrement operator can be placed on both sides (prefix and postfix) of the variable, as demonstrated next:

```
x--;
--x;
```

The next block of code uses the decrement operator in two ways to demonstrate how number-based variables can be decremented by 1:

```
#include <stdio.h>

int main()
{
    int x = 1;
    int y = 1;
```

```
    x = y-- * 4;
    printf("\nThe value of x is %d\n", x);

    y = 1; //reset variable value for demonstration purposes
    x = --y * 4;
    printf("\nThe value of x is now %d\n", x);
    return 0;
}
```

The placement of the decrement operator in each print statement is shown in the output, as illustrated in Figure 4.8.

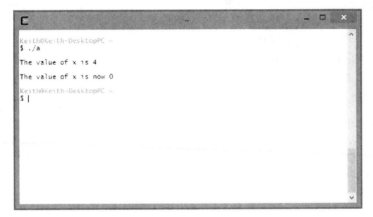

Figure 4.8
Demonstrating decrement operators in both prefix and postfix format.

The += Operator

In this section, you learn about a compound operator (+=) that adds the value of a second variable to the value of the first variable and stores the result in the first variable.

Before I explain further, look at the following expression that assigns one variable's value to another:

```
x = y;
```

The preceding assignment uses a single equal sign to assign the data in the y variable to the x variable. In this case, x does not equal y; rather, x gets y, or x takes on the value of y.

The += operator is also an assignment operator. C provides this friendly assignment operator to increment variables in a new way so that a variable is able to be assigned a new value plus its current value.

To demonstrate its usefulness, see the following line of code, which is an attempt to maintain a running a total without using the newly found += operator:

```
iRunningTotal = iRunningTotal + iNewTotal;
```

Now plug in some numbers to ensure that you understand what is happening. For example, say the iRunningTotal variable contains the number 100 and the variable iNewTotal contains the number 50. Using the preceding statement, what would iRunningTotal be after the statement executed?

If you said 150, you are correct.

The new increment operator (+=) provides a shortcut to solve the same problem. Take another look at the same expression, this time using the += operator:

```
iRunningTotal += iNewTotal;
```

This operator lets you omit unnecessary code when you assign the contents of a variable to another.

Note that it's important to consider order of operations when working with assignment operators. Normal operations such as addition and multiplication have precedence over the increment operator, as demonstrated in the next program:

```c
#include <stdio.h>

int main()
{
    int x = 1;
    int y = 2;

    x = y * x + 1; //arithmetic operations performed before assignment
    printf("\nThe value of x is: %d\n", x);

    x = 1; y = 2;
    x += y * x + 1; //arithmetic operations performed before assignment
    printf("The value of x is: %d\n", x);
    return 0;
} //end main function
```

Demonstrating order of operations, the preceding program displays the following text:

```
The value of x is: 3
The value of x is: 4
```

Although it may seem a bit awkward at first, I'm sure you'll eventually find this assignment operator useful and timesaving.

The -= Operator

The -= operator works similarly to the += operator, but instead of adding a variable's contents to another variable, it subtracts the contents of the variable on the rightmost side of the expression. To demonstrate, study the following statement, which does not use the -= operator:

```
iRunningTotal = iRunningTotal - iNewTotal;
```

You can see from this statement that the variable iRunningTotal is having the value of the iNewTotal variable subtracted from it. You can shorten this statement considerably by using the -= operator, as demonstrated next:

```
iRunningTotal -= iNewTotal;
```

To further demonstrate the -= assignment operator, consider the following program:

```
#include <stdio.h>

int main()
{
    int x = 1;
    int y = 2;

    x = y * x + 1; //arithmetic operations performed before assignment
    printf("\nThe value of x is: %d\n", x);

    x = 1;
    y = 2;
    x -= y * x + 1; //arithmetic operations performed before assignment
    printf("The value of x is: %d\n", x);
    return 0;
} //end main function
```

Using the -= assignment operator in the previous program produces the following output:

```
The value of x is: 3
The value of x is: -2
```

The while Loop

Like all the loops discussed in this chapter, the while loop structure is used to create iteration (loops) in your programs, as demonstrated in the following program:

```
#include <stdio.h>

int main()
{
    int x = 0;

    while ( x < 10 ) {
    printf("The value of x is %d\n", x);
    x++;
    } //end while loop
    return 0;
} //end main function
```

The while statement is summarized like this:

```
while ( x < 10 ) {
```

The while loop uses a condition (in this case x < 10) that evaluates to either true or false. As long as the condition is true, the contents of the loop are executed. Speaking of the loop's contents, you must use the braces to denote the beginning and end of a loop with multiple statements.

Hint

The braces for any loop are required only when more than one statement is included in the loop's body. If your while loop contains only one statement, no braces are required. To demonstrate, look at the following while loop, which does not require the use of braces:

```
while ( x < 10 )
    printf("The value of x is %d\n", x++);
```

In the preceding program, I incremented the variable x by 1 with the increment operator (++). Using this knowledge, how many times do you think the printf() function will execute? To find out, look at Figure 4.9, which depicts the program's output.

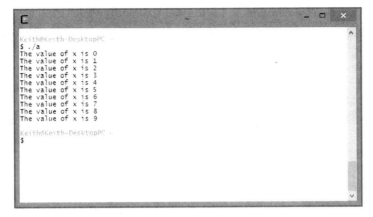

Figure 4.9
Demonstrating the while loop and increment operator (++).

The increment operator (++) is important for this loop. Without it, an endless loop occurs. In other words, the expression x < 10 never evaluates to false, thus creating an infinite loop.

INFINITE LOOPS

Infinite loops are loops that never end. They are created when a loop does not encounter a terminating condition or when a loop is set to restart itself.

Trick

Every programmer experiences an infinite loop at least once in his career. To exit an infinite loop, press Ctrl+C, which produces a break in the program. If this does not work, you may need to end the task.

To end a task on a Windows-based system, press Ctrl+Alt+Delete, which should produce a task window or at least allow you to select the Task Manager. From the Task Manager, select the program that contains the infinite loop and choose End Task.

Loops cause a program to do something repeatedly. Think of an ATM's menu. It always reappears when you complete a transaction. How do you think this happens? You can probably guess by now that the programmers who built the ATM software used a form of iteration.

The following program code demonstrates the `while` loop's usefulness in building menus:

```c
#include <stdio.h>

int main()
{
    int iSelection = 0;

    while ( iSelection != 4 ) {
        printf("1\tDeposit funds\n");
        printf("2\tWithdraw funds\n");
        printf("3\tPrint Balance\n");
        printf("4\tQuit\n");
        printf("Enter your selection (1-4): ");
        scanf("%d", &iSelection);
    } //end while loop

    printf("\nThank you\n");
    return 0;
} //end main function
```

The `while` loop in the preceding program uses a condition to loop as long as the user does not select the number 4. As long as the user selects a valid option other than 4, the menu is displayed repeatedly. If, however, the user selects the number 4, the loop exits and the next statement following the loop's closing brace is executed.

Sample output from the preceding program code is shown in Figure 4.10.

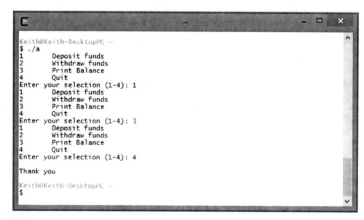

Figure 4.10
Building a menu with the while loop.

The do while Loop

Similar to the while loop, you use the do while loop to build iteration in your programs. The do while loop, however, has a striking difference from the while loop. The do while loop's condition is at the bottom of the loop rather than at the top. To demonstrate, take another look at the first while loop from the previous section, shown next:

```
while ( x < 10 ) {
    printf("The value of x is %d\n", x);
    x++;
} //end while loop
```

The condition is at the beginning of the while loop. The condition of the do while loop, however, is at the end of the loop, as demonstrated next:

```
do {
    printf("The value of x is %d\n", x);
    x++;
} while ( x < 10 ); //end do while loop
```

Trap

In the do while loop's last statement, the ending brace comes before the while statement, and the while statement must end with a semicolon.

If you omit the semicolon or ending brace or simply rearrange the order of syntax, you are guaranteed a compile error.

Studying the preceding do while loop, can you guess how many times the loop will execute and what the output will look like? If you guessed 10 times, you are correct.

Why use the do while loop instead of the while loop? This is a good question, but it can be answered only in relation to the type of problem being solved. I can, however, show you the importance of choosing each of these loops by studying the next program:

```
#include <stdio.h>

int main()
{
    int x = 10;

    do {
```

```
        printf("This printf statement is executed at least once\n");
        x++;
    } while ( x < 10 ); //end do while loop

    while ( x < 10 ) {
        printf("This printf statement is never executed\n");
        x++;
    } //end while loop
    return 0;
} //end main function
```

Using the do while loop enables me to execute the statements inside my loop at least once, even though the loop's condition will be false when evaluated. The while loop's contents, however, never execute because the loop's condition is at the top of the loop and evaluates to false.

The for Loop

The for loop is an important iteration technique in any programming language. Although quite different in syntax from its cousins the while and do while loops, the for loop is much more common for building loops when the number of iterations is already known. The next program block demonstrates a simple for loop:

```
#include <stdio.h>

int main()
{
    int x;

    for ( x = 10; x > 5; x-- )
        printf("The value of x is %d\n", x);
    return 0;
} //end main function
```

The for loop statement is busier than the other loops I've shown you. A single for loop statement contains three separate expressions, as described in the following list:

- Variable initialization
- Conditional expression
- Increment/decrement

Using the preceding code, the first expression, variable initialization, initializes the variable to 10. I did not initialize it in the variable declaration statement because it would have been a duplicated and wasted effort. The next expression is a condition (x > 5) that is used to determine when the for loop should stop iterating. The last expression in the for loop (x--) decrements the variable x by 1.

Using this knowledge, how many times do you think the for loop will execute? If you guessed five times, you are correct.

Figure 4.11 depicts execution of the preceding for loop.

Figure 4.11
Illustrating the for loop.

You can also use the for loop when you don't know how many times the loop should execute. To build a for loop without knowing the number of iterations beforehand, you can, for example, use a user-entered variable as your counter. Take a look at a quiz program that lets the user determine how many questions she would like to answer:

```
#include <stdio.h>
#include <time.h>
#include <stdlib.h>

int main()
{
    int x, iNumQuestions, iResponse, iRndNum1, iRndNum2;
    srand(time(NULL));

    printf("\nEnter number of questions to ask: ");
    scanf("%d", &iNumQuestions);
```

```
for ( x = 0; x < iNumQuestions; x++ ) {
    iRndNum1 = rand() % 10 + 1;
    iRndNum2 = rand() % 10 + 1;
    printf("\nWhat is %d x %d: ", iRndNum1, iRndNum2);
    scanf("%d", &iResponse);
    if ( iResponse == iRndNum1 * iRndNum2 )
        printf("\nCorrect!\n");
    else
        printf("\nThe correct answer was %d \n", iRndNum1 * iRndNum2);
} //end for loop
return 0;
} //end main function
```

In this program code, I first ask the user how many questions she would like to answer. But what I'm really asking is how many times my for loop should execute. I use the number of questions derived from the player in my for loop's condition. Using the variable derived from the user, I can dynamically tell my program how many times to loop.

Sample output for this program is shown in Figure 4.12.

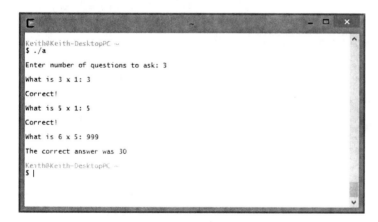

Figure 4.12
Determining the number of iterations with user input.

break and continue Statements

The break and continue statements manipulate program flow in structures such as loops. You may also recall from Chapter 3 that the break statement is used in conjunction with the switch statement.

When a break statement is executed in a loop, the loop is terminated, and program control returns to the next statement following the end of the loop. The next program statements demonstrate the use of the break statement:

```c
#include <stdio.h>

int main()
{
    int x;

    for ( x = 10; x > 5; x-- ) {
    if ( x == 7 )
        break;
} //end for loop

    printf("\n%d\n", x);
    return 0;

}
```

In this program, the condition (x == 7) becomes true after the third iteration. Next, the break statement is executed, and program control is sent out from the for loop and continues with the printf statement.

You also use the continue statement to manipulate program flow in a loop structure. When executed, though, any remaining statements in the loop are passed over, and the next iteration of the loop is sought.

The next program block demonstrates the continue statement:

```c
#include <stdio.h>

int main()
{
    int x;

    for ( x = 10; x > 5; x-- ) {
        if ( x == 7 )
            continue;
        printf("\n%d\n", x);
    } //end for loop
    return 0;

}
```

Notice how the number 7 is not present in the output shown in Figure 4.13. This occurs because, when the condition x == 7 is true, the continue statement is executed, thus skipping the printf() function and continuing program flow with the next iteration of the for loop.

Figure 4.13
Using the continue statement to alter program flow.

System Calls

Many programming languages provide at least one utility function for accessing operating system commands. C provides one such function, called system. You can use the system function to call all types of UNIX or DOS commands from within C program code. For instance, you can call and execute any of the UNIX commands shown in the following list:

- ls
- man
- ps
- pwd

For an explanation of these and other UNIX commands, consult Appendix A, "Common UNIX Commands."

But why call and execute a system command from within a C program? Well, as an example, a common dilemma for programmers of text-based languages, such as C, is how to clear the computer's screen. One solution is shown next:

```c
#include <stdio.h>

int main()
{
    int x;
```

```
    for ( x = 0; x < 25; x++ )
        printf("\n");
    return 0;
} //end main function
```

This program uses a simple `for` loop to repeatedly print a new line character. This eventually clears a computer's screen, but you have to modify it depending on each computer's setting.

A better solution is to use the `system()` function to call the UNIX clear command, as demonstrated next:

```
#include <stdio.h>

int main()
{
    system("clear");
    return 0;
} //end main function
```

Trap

If you get an error message stating that the clear command is not found, go back to the Cygwin setup and install the `ncurses` package, which is under the `Utils` category. The `ncurses` package contains clear.exe and other terminal display utilities.

Using the UNIX clear command provides a more fluid experience for your users and is certainly more discernable when evaluating a programmer's intentions.

Try using various UNIX commands with the `system` function in your own programs. I'm sure you'll find the `system` function to be useful in at least one of your programs.

Chapter Program: Concentration

The Concentration game uses many of the techniques you learned about in this chapter. As shown in Figure 4.14, the game generates random numbers and displays them for a short period for the user to memorize. While the random numbers are displayed, the player should try to memorize the numbers and their sequence. After a few seconds have passed, the screen is cleared, and the user is asked to enter the memorized numbers in the correct sequence.

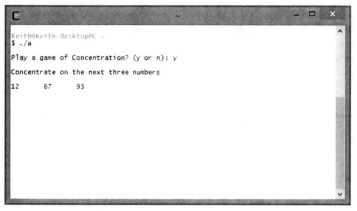

Figure 4.14
Using chapter-based concepts to build the Concentration game.

The complete code for the Concentration game is shown next:

```c
#include <stdio.h>
#include <stdlib.h>
#include <time.h>

int main()
{
    char cYesNo = '\0';
    int iResp1 = 0;
    int iResp2 = 0;
    int iResp3 = 0;
    int iElaspedTime = 0;
    int iCurrentTime = 0;
    int iRandomNum = 0;
    int i1 = 0;
    int i2 = 0;
    int i3 = 0;
    int iCounter = 0;
    srand(time(NULL));

    printf("\nPlay a game of Concentration? (y or n): ");
    scanf("%c", &cYesNo);
```

```
if (cYesNo == 'y' || cYesNo == 'Y') {
    i1 = rand() % 100;
    i2 = rand() % 100;
    i3 = rand() % 100;
    printf("\nConcentrate on the next three numbers\n");
    printf("\n%d\t%d\t%d\n", i1, i2, i3);
    iCurrentTime = time(NULL);
    do {
        iElaspedTime = time(NULL);
    } while ( (iElaspedTime - iCurrentTime) < 3 ); //end do while loop
    system ("clear");
    printf("\nEnter each # separated with one space: ");
    scanf("%d%d%d", &iResp1, &iResp2, &iResp3);
    if ( i1 == iResp1 && i2 == iResp2 && i3 == iResp3 )
    printf("\nCongratulations!\n");
    else
        printf("\nSorry, correct numbers were %d %d %d\n", i1, i2, i3);
} //end if
return 0;
} //end main function
```

Try this game for yourself; I'm certain you and your friends will like it. For more ideas on how to enhance the Concentration game, see the "Challenges" section at the end of this chapter.

Summary

- Looping structures use conditional expressions (conditions) to evaluate how many times something happens.
- You can differentiate between conditions and loops in flowcharts by looking at the program flow. Specifically, if you see connector lines that loop back to the beginning of a condition (diamond symbol), you know that the condition represents a loop.
- The ++ operator is useful for incrementing number-based variables by 1.
- The - - operator decrements number-based variables by 1.
- Both the increment and decrement operators can be placed on both sides (prefix and postfix) of a variable, which produces different results.
- The += operator adds a variable's contents to another variable.
- The -= operator subtracts the contents of a variable from another variable.

- A loop's beginning and ending braces are required only when more than one statement is included in the loop's body.

- Infinite loops are created when a loop's exit condition is never met.

- The do while loop's condition is at the bottom of the loop rather than at the top.

- The for loop is common for building loops when the number of iterations is already known or can be known prior to loop execution.

- When executed, the break statement terminates a loop's execution and returns program control back to the next statement following the end of the loop.

- When executed, the continue statement passes over any remaining statements in the loop and continues to the next iteration in the loop.

- The system() function can be used to call operating system commands such as the UNIX clear command.

Challenges

1. Create a counting program that counts from 1 to 100 in increments of 5.

2. Create a counting program that counts backward from 100 to 1 in increments of 10.

3. Create a counting program that prompts the user for three inputs (shown next) that determine how and what to count. Store the user's answers in variables. Use the acquired data to build your counting program with a for loop and display the results to the user:
   - Beginning number to start counting from
   - Ending number to stop counting at
   - Increment number

4. Create a math quiz program that prompts the user for how many questions to ask. The program should congratulate the player if he gets the correct answer or alert the user of the correct answer if he answers the question incorrectly. The math quiz program should also keep track of how many questions the player has answered correctly and incorrectly and display these running totals at the end of the quiz.

5. Modify the Concentration game to use a main menu. The menu should allow the user to select a level of difficulty or quit the game. (A sample menu is shown next.) The level of difficulty could be determined by how many separate numbers the user has to concentrate on or how many seconds the player has to memorize the sequence of numbers. Each time the user completes a single game of Concentration, the menu should reappear, allowing the user to continue at the same level, continue at a new level, or simply quit the game.
   1. Easy (remember 3 numbers displayed for 5 seconds)
   2. Intermediate (remember 5 numbers displayed for 5 seconds)
   3. Difficult (remember 5 numbers displayed for 2 seconds)
   4. Quit

5

Structured Programming

A concept steeped in computer programming history, *structured programming* enables programmers to break problems into small and easily understood components that eventually comprise a complete system. In this chapter, I show you how to use structured programming concepts, such as top-down design, and programming techniques, such as creating your own functions, to build efficient and reusable code in your programs.

This chapter specifically covers the following topics:

- Introduction to structured programming
- Function prototypes
- Function definitions
- Function calls
- Variable scope
- Chapter program: Trivia

Introduction to Structured Programming

Structured programming enables programmers to break complex systems into manageable components. In C, these components are known as *functions*, which are at the heart of this chapter. In this section, I give you background on common structured programming techniques and concepts. After reading this section, you will be ready to build your own C functions.

Structured programming contains many concepts, ranging from theoretical ideas to practical applications. Many of these concepts are intuitive, whereas others may take a while to sink in and take root.

The most relevant structured programming concepts for this text are the following:

- Top-down design
- Code reusability
- Information hiding

Top-Down Design

Common with procedural languages such as C, *top-down design* enables analysts and programmers to define detailed statements about a system's specific tasks. Top-down design experts argue that humans are limited in their multitasking capabilities. Those who excel at multitasking and enjoy the chaos it brings are generally not programmers. Programmers are inclined to be detail-oriented and work on a single problem at a time.

To demonstrate top-down design, I use an ATM (Automated Teller Machine) as an example. Suppose your nontechnical boss tells you to program the software for an online game's virtual bank. You might wonder where to begin this large and complex task.

Top-down design can help you design your way out of the dark and treacherous forest of systems design. The following steps demonstrate the top-down design process:

1. Break the problem into small, manageable components, starting from the top. In C, the top component is the main() function, from which other components are called.

2. Identify all major components. For the ATM example, assume there are four major components:

   - Display balance
   - Deposit funds
   - Transfer funds
   - Withdraw funds

3. Now that you have separated the major system components, you can visualize the work involved. Break down one major component at a time and make it more manageable and less complex.

4. The "withdraw funds" component can be broken down into smaller pieces, such as these:
   - Get available balance
   - Compare available balance to amount requested
   - Update customer's account
   - Distribute approved funds
   - Reject request
   - Print receipt

5. Go even further with the breaking-down process and divide the "distribute approved funds" component even smaller:
   - Verify that ATM funds exist
   - Initiate (virtual) mechanical processes
   - Update bank records

Figure 5.1 depicts a sample process for breaking down the ATM system.

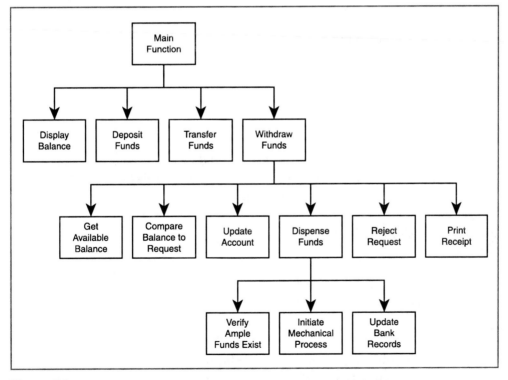

Figure 5.1
Breaking down the ATM system using top-down design.

With my ATM system broken down into manageable components, I feel a bit less feverish about the forthcoming programming tasks. Moreover, I can now assign myself smaller, more manageable components to begin coding.

I hope you see how much easier it is to think about implementing a single component, such as verifying ATM funds exist, than the daunting task of building an entire ATM system. Moreover, when a complex problem is broken down into discreet parts, multiple programmers can work on the same system without knowing the immediate details of each other's programming tasks.

During your programming career, I'm certain you will be faced with similar complex ideas that need to be implemented with programming languages. If used properly, top-down design can be a useful tool for making your problems easier to understand and implement.

Code Reusability

In the world of application development, code reusability is implemented as functions in C. Specifically, programmers create user-defined functions for problems that generally need frequently used solutions. To demonstrate, consider the following list of components and subcomponents from the ATM example in the previous section:

- Get available balance
- Compare available balance to amount requested
- Update customer account
- Distribute approved funds
- Reject request
- Print receipt

Given the ATM system, how many times do you think the "update customer account" problem would occur for any one customer or transaction? Depending on the ATM system, the "update customer account" component can be called a number of times. A customer can perform many transactions while at an ATM. The following list demonstrates possible transactions a customer might perform at a single visit to an ATM:

- Deposit monies into a checking account
- Transfer funds from a checking to a savings account
- Withdraw monies from checking
- Print balance

At least four occasions require you to access the customer's balance. Writing code structures every time you need to access someone's balance doesn't make sense, because you can write a function that contains the logic and structures to handle this procedure and then reuse that function when needed.

Putting all the code into one function that can be called repeatedly saves you programming time immediately and in the future if you need to make changes to the function.

Let me discuss another example using the printf() function (which you are already familiar with) that demonstrates code reuse. In this example, a programmer has already implemented the code and structures needed to print plain text to standard output. You simply use the printf() function by calling its name and passing the desired characters to it. Because the printf() function exists in a module or library, you can call it repeatedly without knowing its implementation details, or, in other words, how it was built. Code reuse is truly a programmer's best friend!

Information Hiding

Information hiding is a conceptual process by which programmers conceal implementation details into functions. Functions can be seen as black boxes. A *black box* is simply a component—logical or physical—that performs a task. You don't know how the black box performs (implements) the task; you just simply know that it works when needed. Figure 5.2 depicts the black box concept.

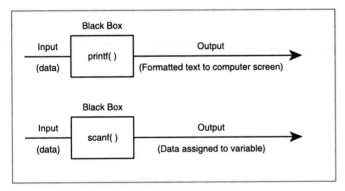

Figure 5.2
Demonstrating the black box concept.

Consider the two black box drawings in Figure 5.2. Each black box describes one component; in this case the components are printf() and scanf(). I consider the two functions printf() and scanf() black boxes because I do not need to know what's inside of them (how they are made); I only need to know what they take as input and what they return as output. In other words, a good example of information hiding is knowing how to use a function but not understanding how it is built.

Many of the functions you have used so far demonstrate the usefulness of information hiding. Table 5.1 lists more common library functions that implement information hiding in structured programming.

TABLE 5.1 COMMON LIBRARY FUNCTIONS

Function	Library Header	Description
scanf()	<stdio.h> (standard input/output)	Reads data from the keyboard
printf()	<stdio.h>	Prints data to the computer monitor
isdigit()	<ctype.h> (character handling)	Tests for decimal digit characters
islower()	<ctype.h>	Tests for lowercase letters
isupper()	<ctype.h>	Tests for uppercase letters
tolower()	<ctype.h>	Converts character to lowercase
toupper()	<ctype.h>	Converts character to uppercase
exp()	<stdio.h>	Computes the exponential
pow()	<math.h> (math functions)	Computes a number raised to a power
sqrt()	<math.h>	Computes the square root

If you're still put off by the notion of information hiding or black boxes, consider the following question: do most people know how a car's engine works? Probably not. Most people are only concerned that they know how to operate a car. Fortunately, modern cars provide an interface from which you can easily use the car while the details of its inner workings are hidden. In other words, you might consider the car's engine the black box. You only know what the black box takes as input (gas) and what it gives as output (motion).

Going back to the printf() function, what do you really know about it? You know that the printf() function prints characters you supply to the computer's screen. But do you know how the printf() function really works? Probably not, and you don't need to. That's a key concept of information hiding.

In structured programming, you build components that can be reused (code reusability) and that include an interface that other programmers will know how to use without needing to understand how they were built (information hiding).

Function Prototypes

Function prototypes tell C how your functions are to be built and used. It is a common programming practice to construct your function prototype before the actual function is built. That's an important concern, so it is worth noting again: *It is common programming practice to construct your function prototype before the actual function is built.*

Programmers must think about the desired purpose of the function, how it will receive input, and how and what it will return. To demonstrate, look at the following function prototype:

```
float addTwoNumbers(int, int);
```

This function prototype tells C the following things about the function:

- The data type returned by the function—in this case, a float data type is returned
- The number of parameters received—in this case, two
- The data types of the parameters—in this case, both parameters are integer data types
- The order of the parameters

Function implementations and their prototypes can vary. It is not always necessary to send input as parameters to functions, nor is it always necessary to have functions return values. In these cases, programmers say the functions are void of parameters or are void of a return value. The next two function prototypes demonstrate the concept of functions with the void keyword:

```
void printBalance(int); //function prototype
```

The void keyword in the preceding example tells C that the function printBalance will not return a value. In other words, this function is void of a return value:

```
int createRandomNumber(void); //function prototype
```

The void keyword in the parameter list of the createRandomNumber function tells C this function will not accept parameters, but it will return an integer value. In other words, this function is void of parameters.

You should place function prototypes outside the main() function and before the main() function starts, as demonstrated next:

```
#include <stdio.h>

int addTwoNumbers(int, int); //function prototype

int main()
{
}
```

There is no limit to the number of function prototypes you can include in your C program. Consider the next block of code, which implements four function prototypes:

```
#include <stdio.h>
```

```
int addTwoNumbers(int, int); //function prototype
int subtractTwoNumbers(int, int); //function prototype
int divideTwoNumbers(int, int); //function prototype
int multiplyTwoNumbers(int, int); //function prototype

int main()
{
}
```

Function Definitions

I have shown you how C programmers create the blueprints for user-defined functions with function prototypes. In this section, I show you how to build user-defined functions using the function prototypes.

Function definitions implement the function prototype. In fact, the first line of the function definition (also known as the *header*) resembles the function prototype, with minor variations. To demonstrate, study the next block of code:

```
#include <stdio.h>

int addTwoNumbers(int, int); //function prototype

int main()
{
    printf("Nothing happening in here.");
    return 0;
}

//function definition
int addTwoNumbers(int operand1, int operand2)
{
    return operand1 + operand2;
}
```

I have two separate and complete functions: the main() function and the addTwoNumbers() function. The function prototype and the first line of the function definition (the function header) are quite similar. The only difference is that the function header contains actual variable names for parameters, and the function prototype contains only the variable data type. The function definition does not contain a semicolon after the header (unlike its prototype). As with the main() function, the function definition must include a beginning and ending brace.

In C, functions can return a value to the calling statement. To return a value, use the return keyword, which initiates the return value process. In the next section, you learn how to call a function that receives its return value.

Trick

You can use the keyword return in one of two fashions: first, you can use the return keyword to pass a value or expression result back to the calling statement. Second, you can use the keyword return without values or expressions to send program control back to the calling statement.

Sometimes, however, it is not necessary for a function to return a value. For example, the next program builds a function simply to compare the values of two numbers:

```c
//function definition
int compareTwoNumbers(int num1, int num2)
{
    if (num1 < num2)
        printf("\n%d is less than %d\n", num1, num2);
    else if (num1 == num2)
        printf("\n%d is equal to %d\n", num1, num2);
    else
        printf("\n%d is greater than %d\n", num1, num2);
}
```

Notice in the preceding function definition that the function compareTwoNumbers() does not return a value. To further demonstrate the process of building functions, study the next program that builds a report header:

```c
//function definition
void printReportHeader()
{
    printf("\nColumn1\tColumn2\tColumn3\tColumn4\n");
}
```

To build a program that implements multiple function definitions, build each function definition as stated in each function prototype. The next program implements the main() function, which does nothing of importance, and then builds two functions to perform basic math operations and return a result:

```c
#include <stdio.h>

int addTwoNumbers(int, int); //function prototype
int subtractTwoNumbers(int, int); //function prototype

int main()
{
    printf("Nothing happening in here.");
    return 0;
}

//function definition
int addTwoNumbers(int num1, int num2)
{
    return num1 + num2;
}

//function definition
int subtractTwoNumbers(int num1, int num2)
{
    return num1 - num2;
}
```

Function Calls

It's now time to put your functions to work with function calls. Up to this point, you may have been wondering how you or your program would use these functions. You work with your user-defined functions the same way you work with other C library functions such as printf() and scanf().

Using the addTwoNumbers() function from the previous section, I include a single function call in my main() function, as shown next:

```c
#include <stdio.h>

int addTwoNumbers(int, int); //function prototype

int main()
{
    int iResult;
```

```
    iResult = addTwoNumbers(5, 5); //function call
    return 0;
}


//function definition
int addTwoNumbers(int operand1, int operand2)
{
    return operand1 + operand2;
}
```

addTwoNumbers(5, 5) calls the function and passes it two integer parameters. When C encounters a function call, it redirects program control to the function definition. If the function definition returns a value, the entire function call statement is replaced by the return value.

In other words, the entire statement addTwoNumbers(5, 5) is replaced with the number 10. In the preceding program, the returned value of 10 is assigned to the integer variable iResult.

Function calls can also be placed in other functions. To demonstrate, study the next block of code that uses the same addTwoNumbers() function call inside a printf() function:

```
#include <stdio.h>


int addTwoNumbers(int, int); //function prototype


int main()
{
    printf("\nThe result is %d", addTwoNumbers(5, 5));
    return 0;
}


//function definition
int addTwoNumbers(int operand1, int operand2)
{
    return operand1 + operand2;
}
```

In the preceding function call, I hard-coded two numbers as parameters. You can be more dynamic with function calls by passing variables as parameters, as shown next:

```
#include <stdio.h>


int addTwoNumbers(int, int); //function prototype
```

```
int main()
{
    int num1, num2;

    printf("\nEnter the first number: ");
    scanf("%d", &num1);

    printf("\nEnter the second number: ");
    scanf("%d", &num2);

    printf("\nThe result is %d\n", addTwoNumbers(num1, num2));
    return 0;
}


//function definition
int addTwoNumbers(int operand1, int operand2)
{
    return operand1 + operand2;
}
```

The output of the preceding program is shown in Figure 5.3.

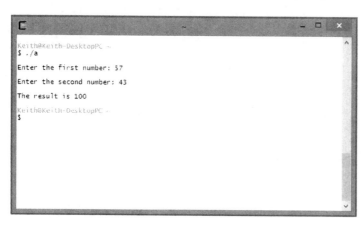

Figure 5.3
Passing variables as parameters to user-defined functions.

Demonstrated next is the printReportHeader() function, which prints a report header using the \t escape sequence to print a tab between words:

```
#include <stdio.h>

void printReportHeader(); //function prototype

int main()
{
    printReportHeader();
    return 0;
}

//function definition
void printReportHeader()
{
    printf("\nColumn1\tColumn2\tColumn3\tColumn4\n");
}
```

Calling a function that requires no parameters or returns no value is as simple as calling its name with empty parentheses.

Trap

Failing to use parentheses in function calls void of parameters can result in compile errors or invalid program operations. Consider the two following function calls:

```
printReportHeader; //Incorrect function call
printReportHeader(); //Correct function call
```

The first function call does not cause a compile error but fails to execute the function call to printReportHeader. The second function call, however, contains the empty parentheses and successfully calls printReportHeader().

Variable Scope

Variable scope identifies and determines the life span of any variable in any programming language. When a variable loses its scope, its data value is lost. I discuss two common types of variables scopes in C—local and global—so you will better understand the importance of variable scope.

Local Scope

You have unknowingly been using local scope variables since Chapter 2, "Primary Data Types." Local variables are defined in functions, such as the main() function, and lose their scope each time the function is executed, as shown in the following program:

```c
#include <stdio.h>

int main()
{
    int num1;

    printf("\nEnter a number: ");
    scanf("%d", &num1);

    printf("\nYou entered %d\n ", num1);
    return 0;
}
```

Each time the preceding program is run, C allocates memory space for the integer variable num1 with its variable declaration. Data stored in the variable is lost when the main() function is terminated.

Because local scope variables are tied to their originating functions, you can reuse variable names in other functions without running the risk of overwriting data. To demonstrate, review the following program code and its output in Figure 5.4:

```c
#include <stdio.h>

int getSecondNumber(); //function prototype

int main()
{
    int num1;

    printf("\nEnter a number: ");
    scanf("%d", &num1);

    printf("\nYou entered %d and %d\n ", num1, getSecondNumber());
    return 0;
}
```

```
//function definition
int getSecondNumber ()
{
    int num1;

    printf("\nEnter a second number: ");
    scanf("%d", &num1);
    return num1;
}
```

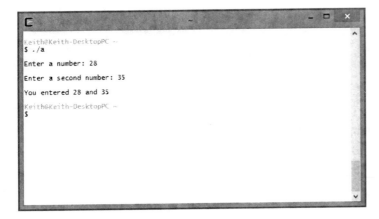

Figure 5.4
Using the same local scope variable
name in different functions.

Because the variable num1 is scoped locally to each function, there are no concerns or issues with overwriting data. Specifically, the num1 variable in each function is a separate memory address; therefore, each is a unique variable.

Global Scope

You can reuse locally scoped variables in other functions without harming one another's contents. At times, however, you might want to share data between and across functions. To support the concept of sharing data, you can create and use *global variables*.

Global variables are created and defined outside any function, including the main() function. To learn how global variables work, examine the next program:

```
#include <stdio.h>

void printLuckyNumber(); //function prototype
int iLuckyNumber; //global variable
```

```
int main()
{
    printf("\nEnter your lucky number: ");
    scanf("%d", &iLuckyNumber);

    printLuckyNumber();
    return 0;
}


//function definition
void printLuckyNumber()
{
    printf("\nYour lucky number is: %d\n", iLuckyNumber);
}
```

The variable iLuckyNumber is global because it is created outside any function, including the main() function. You can assign data to the global variable in one function and reference the same memory space in another function. It is not wise, however, to overuse global variables, because they can easily be modified by any function and thus lead to erroneous data. Use proper scope to protect your data, and follow the principles of information hiding.

Chapter Program: Trivia

As demonstrated in Figure 5.5, the Trivia game utilizes many of this chapter's concepts and techniques.

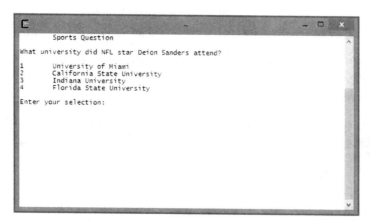

Figure 5.5
Demonstrating chapter-based concepts with the Trivia game.

The Trivia game uses function prototypes, function definitions, function calls, and a global variable to build a simple and fun game. Players select a trivia category from the main menu and are asked a question. The program replies that the answer is correct or incorrect.

Each trivia category is broken down into a function that implements the question-and-answer logic. There is also a user-defined function that builds a pause utility.

All the code necessary for building the Trivia game is shown next:

```c
#include <stdio.h>
#include <time.h>
#include <stdlib.h>


/*********************************************
FUNCTION PROTOTYPES
*********************************************/
int sportsQuestion(void);
int geographyQuestion(void);
void pause(int);


/*********************************************
GLOBAL VARIABLE
*********************************************/
int giResponse = 0;


/*********************************************/
  int main()
  {
  do {
      system("clear");
      printf("\n\tTHE TRIVIA GAME\n\n");
      printf("1\tSports\n");
      printf("2\tGeography\n");
      printf("3\tQuit\n");
      printf("\n\nEnter your selection: ");
      scanf("%d", &giResponse);

      switch(giResponse) {
          case 1:
              if (sportsQuestion() == 4)
                  printf("\nCorrect!\n");
```

```c
                else
                    printf("\nIncorrect\n");
                pause(2);
                break;
            case 2:
                if (geographyQuestion() == 2)
                    printf("\nCorrect!\n");
                else
                    printf("\nIncorrect\n");
                pause(2);
                break;
        } //end switch
    } while ( giResponse != 3 );
    return 0;
} //end main function


/************************************************************
FUNCTION DEFINITION
************************************************************/
int sportsQuestion(void)
{
    int iAnswer = 0;
    system("clear");
    printf("\tSports Question\n");
    printf("\nWhat university did NFL star Deion Sanders attend? ");
    printf("\n\n1\tUniversity of Miami\n");
    printf("2\tCalifornia State University\n");
    printf("3\tIndiana University\n");
    printf("4\tFlorida State University\n");
    printf("\nEnter your selection: ");
    scanf("%d", &iAnswer);
    return iAnswer;
} //end sportsQuestion function


/************************************************************
FUNCTION DEFINITION
************************************************************/
int geographyQuestion(void)
{
```

```
        int iAnswer = 0;
        system("clear");
        printf("\tGeography Question\n");
        printf("\nWhat is the state capital of Florida? ");
        printf("\n\n1\tPensacola\n");
        printf("2\tTallahassee\n");
        printf("3\tJacksonville\n");
        printf("4\tMiami\n");
        printf("\nEnter your selection: ");
        scanf("%d", &iAnswer);
        return iAnswer;
} //end geographyQuestion function


/***********************************************************
FUNCTION DEFINITION
***********************************************************/
void pause(int inNum)
{
        int iCurrentTime = 0;
        int iElapsedTime = 0;
        iCurrentTime = time(NULL);
        do {
            iElapsedTime = time(NULL);
        } while ( (iElapsedTime - iCurrentTime) < inNum );
} //end pause function
```

Summary

- Structured programming enables programmers to break complex systems into manageable components.
- Top-down design breaks the problem into small, manageable components, starting from the top.
- Code reusability is implemented as functions in C.
- Information hiding is a conceptual process by which programmers conceal implementation details into functions.
- Function prototypes tell C how your function will be built and used.
- It is common programming practice to construct your function prototype before the actual function is built.

- Function prototypes tell C the data type returned by the function, the number of parameters received, the data types of the parameters, and the order of the parameters.
- Function definitions implement the function prototype.
- In C, functions can return a value to the calling statement. To return a value, use the `return` keyword, which initiates the return value process.
- You can use the `return` keyword to pass a value or expression result to the calling statement, or you can use the keyword `return` without values or expressions to return program control to the calling statement.
- Failing to use parentheses in function calls void of parameters can result in compile errors or invalid program operations.
- Variable scope identifies and determines the life span of any variable in any programming language. When a variable loses its scope, it loses its data value.
- Local variables are defined in functions, such as `main()`, and lose their scope each time the function is executed.
- Locally scoped variables can be reused in other functions without harming one another's contents.
- Global variables are created and defined outside any function, including the `main()` function.

Challenges

1. Write a function prototype for the following components:
   - A function that divides two numbers and returns the remainder
   - A function that finds the larger of two numbers and returns the result
   - A function that prints an ATM menu—it receives no parameters and returns no value
2. Build the function definitions for each preceding function prototype.
3. Add your own trivia categories to the Trivia game.
4. Modify the Trivia game to track the number of times a user gets an answer correct and incorrect. When the user quits the program, display the number of correct and incorrect answers. Consider using global variables to track the number of questions answered, the number answered correctly, and the number answered incorrectly.

Arrays

A rrays are an important and versatile programming construct, enabling you to build and work with a large amount of related data (data that is of the same type) in a structured way using one name to reference the entire set of data.

This chapter covers many array topics, such as creating single and multidimensional arrays, initializing them, and searching through their contents. Specifically, this chapter covers the following array topics:

- Introduction to arrays
- One-dimensional arrays
- Two-dimensional arrays
- Chapter program: Tic-Tac-Toe

Introduction to Arrays

Just as with loops and conditions, arrays are a common programming construct and an important concept for beginning programmers to learn. Arrays can be found in most high-level programming languages, such as C, and offer a simple way of grouping like variables for easy access. Arrays in C share a few common attributes:

- Variables in an array share the same name.
- Variables in an array share the same data type.
- Individual variables in an array are called *elements.*
- Elements in an array are accessed with an index number.

Like any other variable, arrays occupy memory space. Moreover, an array is a grouping of contiguous memory segments, as demonstrated in Figure 6.1.

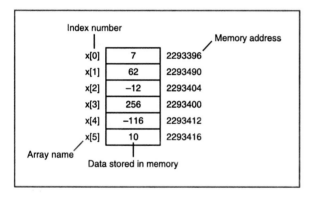

Figure 6.1
A six-element array.

The six-element array in Figure 6.1 starts with index 0. This is an important concept to remember, so it's worth repeating. *Elements in an array begin with index number zero.* There are six array elements in Figure 6.1, starting with element 0 and ending with element 5.

Trap

A common programming error is to not account for the zero-based index in arrays. This programming error is often called the *off-by-one error.* This type of error is generally not caught during compile time, but rather at run time when a user or your program attempts to access an element number of an array that does not exist. For example, if you have a six-element array and your program tries to access the sixth element with index number six, either a run-time program error ensues or data is lost. This is because the last index in a six-element array is index 5.

One-Dimensional Arrays

Sometimes you might need or want to use a one-dimensional array. Although there is no rule for when to use an array, some problems are better suited for an array-based solution, as demonstrated in the following list:

- The number of pages in each chapter of a book
- A list of students' GPAs
- Your golf score history
- A list of phone numbers

Looking at the preceding list, you may be wondering why you would use an array to store the aforementioned information. Consider the golf score statement. If you created a program that kept track of your golf scores, how many variables, or better yet variable names, would you need to store a score for each hole in a golf game? If you solved this question with individual variables, your variable declarations may resemble the following code:

```
int iHole1, iHole2, iHole3, iHole4, iHole5, iHole6;
int iHole7, iHole8, iHole9, iHole10, iHole11, iHole12;
int iHole13, iHole14, iHole15, iHole16, iHole17, iHole18;
```

Whew! That's a lot of variables to keep track of. If you use an array, you only need one variable name with 18 elements, as shown next.

```
int iGolfScores[18];
```

Creating One-Dimensional Arrays

Creating and using one-dimensional arrays is easy, although it may take some time and practice for it to become that way. Arrays in C are created in similar fashion to other variables, as shown next:

```
int iArray[10];
```

The preceding declaration creates a single-dimension, integer-based array called iArray, which contains 10 elements. Remember that arrays are zero-based; you start counting with the number zero up to the number defined in the brackets minus 1 (0, 1, 2, 3, 4, 5, 6, 7, 8, 9 gives you 10 elements).

Arrays can be declared to contain other data types as well. To demonstrate, consider the next array declarations using various data types:

```
float fAverages[30]; //Float data type array with 30 elements
double dResults[3]; //Double data type array with 3 elements
short sSalaries[9]; //Short data type array with 9 elements
char cName[19]; //Char array - 18 character elements and one NULL character
```

Initializing One-Dimensional Arrays

In C, memory spaces are not cleared from their previous value when variables or arrays are created. Because of this, it is generally good programming practice to not only initialize your variables but also initialize your arrays.

There are two ways to initialize your arrays: within the array declaration and outside the array declaration. In the first way, you simply assign one or more comma-separated values within braces to the array in the array's declaration:

```c
int iArray[5] = {0, 1, 2, 3, 4};
```

Placing numbers inside braces and separating them by commas assigns a default value to each respective element number.

Trick

You can quickly initialize your arrays with a single default value, as demonstrated in the following array declaration:

```c
int iArray[5] = {0};
```

Assigning the single numeric value of 0 in an array declaration will, by default, assign all array elements the value of 0.

Another way to initialize your array elements is to use looping structures such as the for loop. To demonstrate, examine the following program code:

```c
#include <stdio.h>

int main()
{
    int x;
    int iArray[5];

    for ( x = 0; x < 5; x++ )
        iArray[x] = 0;
    return 0;
}
```

In the preceding program, I've declared two variables: one integer variable called x, which is used in the for loop, and one integer-based array called iArray. Because I know I have five elements in my array, I need to iterate five times in my for loop. Within my loop, I assign the number zero to each element of the array; the elements are easily accessed with the counter variable x inside my assignment statement.

To print the entire contents of an array, you also need to use a looping structure, as demonstrated in the next program:

```c
#include <stdio.h>

int main()
{
    int x;
    int iArray[5];

//initialize array elements
    for ( x = 0; x < 5; x++ )
        iArray[x] = x;

//print array element contents
    for ( x = 0; x < 5; x++ )
        printf("\nThe value of iArray index %d is %d\n", x, x);
    return 0;
}
```

I initialize the preceding array called iArray differently by assigning the value of the x variable to each array element. I get a different value for each array element, as shown in Figure 6.2, because the x variable is incremented each time the loop iterates. After initializing the array, I use another for loop to print the contents of the array.

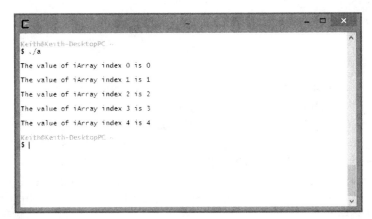

Figure 6.2
Printing the contents of an array.

Sometimes you only need to access a single element of an array, which you can do in one of two ways: hard-coding a number value for the index or using variables. Hard-coding a number value for the index is shown in the next printf() function:

```
printf("\nThe value of index 4 is %d\n", iArray[3]);
```

Hard-coding the index value of an array assumes that you will always need or want the element number. A more dynamic way of accessing a single element number is to use variables. In the next program block, I use the input of a user to access a single array element's value:

```c
#include <stdio.h>

int main()
{
    int x;
    int iIndex = -1;
    int iArray[5];

    for ( x = 0; x < 5; x++ )
    iArray[x] = (x + 5);

    do {
        printf("\nEnter a valid index (0-4): ");
        scanf("%d", &iIndex);
    } while ( iIndex < 0 || iIndex > 4 );

    printf("\nThe value of index %d is %d\n", iIndex, iArray[iIndex]);
    return 0;
} //end main
```

I mix up the array initialization in the for loop by adding the integer 5 to the value of x each time the loop iterates. I must perform more work, however, when getting an index value from the user. Basically, I test that the user has entered a valid index number; otherwise, my program provides invalid results. To validate the user's input, I insert printf() and scanf() functions inside a do while loop and iterate until I get a valid value, after which I can print the desired element contents. Figure 6.3 demonstrates the output of the preceding program block when run on my computer. Because the first part of the program prints whatever happens to be in memory for the uninitialized array, your results will be different.

You should initialize character arrays before using them. Elements in a character array hold characters plus a special NULL termination character, which is represented by the character constant '\0'.

You can initialize character arrays in a number of ways. For instance, the following code initializes an array with a predetermined character sequence:

```
char cName[] = { 'O', 'l', 'i', 'v', 'i', 'a', '\0' };
```

Figure 6.3
Accessing one element of an array with a variable.

The preceding array declaration creates an array called cName with seven elements, including the NULL character '\0'. Another way of initializing the same cName array is revealed next:

```
char cName[] = "Olivia";
```

Initializing a character array with a character sequence surrounded by double quotes appends the NULL character automatically.

Trap

When creating character arrays, be sure to allocate enough room to store the largest character sequence assignable. Also, remember to allow enough room in the character array to store the NULL character ('\0').

Study the next program, with output shown in Figure 6.4. It demonstrates the creation of two character arrays—one initialized and the other not.

```
#include <stdio.h>

int main()
{
```

```
    int x;
    char cArray[5]; // uninitialized array
    char cName[] = "Olivia"; // initialized array

    printf("\nUninitialized character array (contains unintended data):\n");
    for ( x = 0; x < 5; x++ )
        printf("cArray[%d] contains value %d\n", x, cArray[x]);

    printf("\nInitialized character array (contains intended data):\n");
    for ( x = 0; x < 6; x++ )
        printf("%c", cName[x]);
    return 0;
} //end main
```

Figure 6.4 demonstrates why it is necessary to initialize arrays. An uninitialized array contains data—just not the data you want. You may have noticed that in the preceding program, I printed the contents of the uninitialized array as integers. Why? Because it is unlikely that some of the contents could even be displayed as characters. In the case of Figure 6.4, you can see leftover data (not assigned or initialized by me) stored in the elements of cArray.

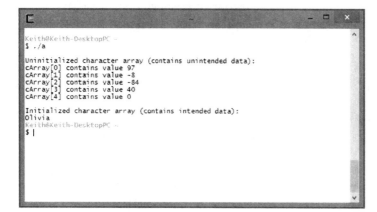

Figure 6.4
Initializing a character-based array.

Searching One-Dimensional Arrays

One of the most common practices with arrays is searching their elements for contents. Once again, you will use looping structures, such as the for loop, to iterate through each element until the search value is found or the search is over.

The concept of searching an array is demonstrated in the next program, which prompts a user to enter a numeric search value:

```c
#include <stdio.h>

int main()
{
    int x;
    int iValue;
    int iFound = -1;
    int iArray[5];

    for ( x = 0; x < 5; x++ )
        iArray[x] = (x + x); //initialize array

    printf("\nEnter value to search for: ");
    scanf("%d", &iValue);

    for ( x = 0; x < 5; x++ ) {
        if ( iArray[x] == iValue ) {
            iFound = x;
            break;
        }
    } //end for loop

    if ( iFound > -1 )
        printf("\nI found your search value in element %d\n", iFound);
    else
        printf("\nSorry, your search value was not found\n");
    return 0;
} //end main
```

As the preceding program shows, I use two separate loops: one for initializing my integer-based array to the counting variable plus itself (iArray[x] = (x + x)) and the other, which searches the array using the user's search value.

Valid values for each preceding array element are shown in Table 6.1.

TABLE 6.1 VALID ELEMENT VALUES FOR iArray[X] = (X + X)	
Element Number	**Value After Initialization**
0	0
1	2
2	4
3	6
4	8

If a match is found, I assign the element to a variable and exit the loop with the break keyword. After the search process, I alert the user if the value was found and where (at which element number). I also alert the user if no match was found.

Figure 6.5 demonstrates the output of the searching program.

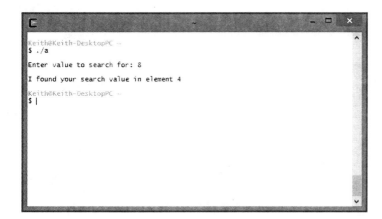

Figure 6.5
Searching the contents of an array.

Remember that you can use the break keyword to exit a loop early. When C encounters the break keyword in a loop, it moves program control to the next statement outside of the loop. This can be a timesaving advantage when searching through large amounts of information.

Two-Dimensional Arrays

Two-dimensional arrays are even more interesting structures than their single-dimension counterparts. The easiest way to understand or think about two-dimensional arrays is to visualize a table with rows and columns (such as a checkerboard, chessboard, or spreadsheet). C, however, implements two-dimensional arrays as single-dimension arrays with pointers to other single-dimension arrays. For the sake of simplicity, however, you can visualize two-dimensional arrays as a grid or table, as mentioned.

Two-dimensional arrays are created similarly to one-dimensional arrays, but with one exception: two-dimensional arrays must be declared with two separate element numbers (number of columns and number of rows), as shown next:

```
int iTwoD[3][3];
```

The preceding array declaration creates a total of 9 elements. (Remember that array indexes start with number 0.) You access two-dimensional arrays with two element numbers: one for the column and one for the row.

Figure 6.6 demonstrates a two-dimensional array with nine elements.

	Column 0	Column 1	Column 2
Row 0	iTwoD[0][0]	iTwoD[0][1]	iTwoD[0][2]
Row 1	iTwoD[1][0]	iTwoD[1][1]	iTwoD[1][2]
Row 2	iTwoD[2][0]	iTwoD[2][1]	iTwoD[2][2]

Figure 6.6
Two-dimensional array described.

Initializing Two-Dimensional Arrays

You can initialize a two-dimensional array in a couple of ways. First, you can initialize a two-dimensional array in its declaration, as shown next:

```
int iTwoD[3][3] = { {0, 1, 2}, {1, 2, 3}, {2, 3, 4} };
```

Each grouping of braces initializes a single row of elements. For example, `iTwoD[0][0]` gets 0, `iTwoD[1][1]` gets 2, and `iTwoD[3][2]` gets 4. Table 6.2 demonstrates all the values assigned to the preceding two-dimensional array.

Table 6.2 Two-Dimensional Array Values After Initializing

Element Reference	Value	Element Reference	Value
iTwoD[0][0]	0	iTwoD[1][2]	3
iTwoD[0][1]	1	iTwoD[2][0]	2
iTwoD[0][2]	2	iTwoD[2][1]	3
iTwoD[1][0]	1	iTwoD[2][2]	4
iTwoD[1][1]	2		

You can also use looping structures, such as the `for` loop, to initialize your two-dimensional arrays. As you might expect, there is a bit more work when initializing or searching a two-dimensional array. Essentially, you must create a nested looping structure for searching or accessing each element, as shown in the next program:

```c
#include <stdio.h>

int main()
{
    int iTwoD[3][3];
    int x, y;

    //initialize the 2D array
    for ( x = 0; x <= 2; x++ ) {
        for ( y = 0; y <= 2; y++ )
            iTwoD[x][y] = ( x + y );
    } //end outer loop

    //print the 2D array
    for ( x = 0; x <= 2; x++ ) {
        for ( y = 0; y <= 2; y++ )
            printf("iTwoD[%d][%d] = %d\n", x, y, iTwoD[x][y]);
    } //end outer loop
    return 0;
} //end main
```

Nested loops are necessary to search through a two-dimensional array. In the preceding example, my first combination of looping structures initializes each element to variable x plus variable y. Moreover, the outer loop controls the number of iterations through the rows (three rows in all). Once inside the first loop, my inner loop takes over and iterates three times for each outer loop. The inner loop uses a separate variable, y, to loop through each column number of the current row (three columns in each row). The last grouping of loops accesses each element and prints to standard output using the `printf()` function.

The output of the preceding program is shown in Figure 6.7.

Looping through two-dimensional arrays with nested loops can certainly be a daunting task for the beginning programmer. My best advice is to practice, practice, and practice! The more you program, the clearer the concepts become.

Figure 6.7
Initializing a two-dimensional array with nested loops.

Searching Two-Dimensional Arrays

The concept behind searching a two-dimensional array is similar to that of searching a single-dimension array. You must receive a searchable value, such as user input, and then search the array's contents until you find a value or you search the entire array without a match.

When searching two-dimensional arrays, however, you must use the nested looping techniques I described in the previous section. The nested looping constructs enable you to search each array element individually.

The following program demonstrates how to search a two-dimensional array:

```
#include <stdio.h>

int main()
{
    int iTwoD[3][3] = { {1, 2, 3}, {4, 5, 6}, {7, 8, 9} };
    int iFoundAt[2] = {0, 0};
    int x, y;
    int iValue = 0;
    int iFound = 0;

    printf("\nEnter a search value from 1 to 9: ");
    scanf("%d", &iValue);

    //search the 2D array
    for ( x = 0; x <= 2; x++ ) {
```

```
    for ( y = 0; y <= 2; y++ ) {
        if ( iTwoD[x][y] == iValue ) { iFound = 1;
            iFoundAt[0] = x;
            iFoundAt[1] = y;
            break;
        } //end if
    } //end inner loop
} //end outer loop

if ( iFound == 1 )
printf("\nFound value in iTwoD[%d][%d]\n", iFoundAt[0], iFoundAt[1]);
else
    printf("\nValue not found\n");
return 0;
} //end main
```

The architecture of the preceding nested looping structure is a reoccurring theme when dealing with two-dimensional arrays. More specifically, you must use two loops to search a two-dimensional array: one loop to search the rows and an inner loop to search each column for the outer loop's row.

In addition to using the multidimensional array, I use a single-dimension array, called iFoundAt, to store the row and column location of the two-dimensional array if I find the search value. If I find the search value, I want to let the user know where I found his value.

The output of the searchable two-dimensional array program is shown in Figure 6.8.

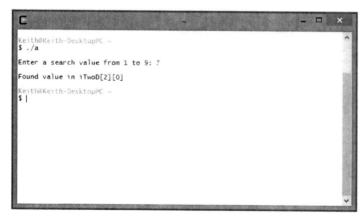

Figure 6.8
Searching a two-dimensional array with nested loops.

Chapter Program: Tic-Tac-Toe

The Tic-Tac-Toe game, as shown in Figure 6.9, is a fun and easy way to demonstrate the techniques and array data structures you learned about in this chapter. Moreover, the Tic-Tac-Toe game uses techniques and programming structures that you learned in previous chapters, such as function prototypes, definitions, system calls, and global variables.

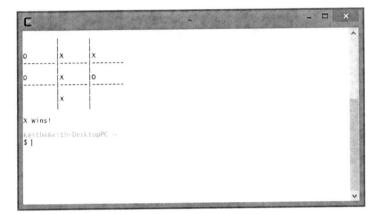

Figure 6.9
Tic-Tac-Toe as the chapter-based game.

A total of four functions, including the main() function, are used to build the Tic-Tac-Toe game. Table 6.3 describes each function's purpose.

TABLE 6.3 FUNCTIONS USED IN THE TIC-TAC-TOE GAME	
Function Name	**Function Description**
main()	Initializes array and prompts players for X and O placement until the game is over
displayBoard()	Clears the screen and displays the board with X and O placements
verifySelection()	Verifies that square is empty before placing an X or O inside the square
checkForWin()	Checks for a win by X or O or a tie (cat) game

All the code required to build the Tic-Tac-Toe game is shown next:

```
#include <stdio.h>
#include <stdlib.h>


/*******************************
function prototypes
```

```
*********************************/
void displayBoard();
int verifySelection(int, int);
void checkForWin();

/******************
global variables
*****************/
char board[8];
char cWhoWon = ' ';
int iCurrentPlayer = 0;

/**********************************************************
begin main function
**********************************************************/
int main() {
    int x;
    int iSquareNum = 0;

    for ( x = 0; x < 9; x++ )
        board[x] = ' ';
    displayBoard();

    while ( cWhoWon == ' ') {
        printf("\n%c\n", cWhoWon);
        if ( iCurrentPlayer == 1 || iCurrentPlayer == 0 ) {
            printf("\nPLAYER X\n");
            printf("Enter an available square number (1-9): ");
            scanf("%d", &iSquareNum);
            if ( verifySelection(iSquareNum, iCurrentPlayer) == 1 )
                iCurrentPlayer = 1;
            else
                iCurrentPlayer = 2;
        }
        else {
            printf("\nPLAYER O\n");
            printf("Enter an available square number (1-9): ");
            scanf("%d", &iSquareNum);
            if ( verifySelection(iSquareNum, iCurrentPlayer) == 1 )
```

```
                        iCurrentPlayer = 2;
                else
                        iCurrentPlayer = 1;
        } // end if
        displayBoard();
        checkForWin();
    } //end loop
    return 0;
} //end main function


/*************************************************************
begin function definition
*************************************************************/
void displayBoard() {
    system("clear");
    printf("\n\t|\t|\n");
    printf("\t|\t|\n");
    printf("%c\t|%c\t|%c\n", board[0], board[1], board[2]);
    printf("----|-----|----\n");
    printf("\t|\t|\n");
    printf("%c\t|%c\t|%c\n", board[3], board[4], board[5]);
    printf("----|----—|----\n");
    printf("\t|\t|\n");
    printf("%c\t|%c\t|%c\n", board[6], board[7], board[8]);
    printf("\t|\t|\n");
} //end function definition


/*************************************************************
begin function definition
*************************************************************/
int verifySelection(int iSquare, int iPlayer) {
    if ( board[iSquare - 1] == ' ' && (iPlayer == 1 || iPlayer == 0) ) {
        board[iSquare - 1] = 'X';
        return 0;
    }
    else if ( board[iSquare - 1] == ' ' && iPlayer == 2 ) {
        board[iSquare - 1] = '0';
        return 0;
    }
```

```
    else
        return 1;
} //end function definition

/**********************************************************
begin function definition
**********************************************************/
void checkForWin() {
    int catTotal;
    int x;

    if (board[0] == 'X' && board[1] == 'X' && board[2] == 'X')
        cWhoWon = 'X';
    else if (board[3] == 'X' && board[4] == 'X' && board[5] == 'X')
        cWhoWon = 'X';
    else if (board[6] == 'X' && board[7] == 'X' && board[8] == 'X')
        cWhoWon = 'X';
    else if (board[0] == 'X' && board[3] == 'X' && board[6] == 'X')
        cWhoWon = 'X';
    else if (board[1] == 'X' && board[4] == 'X' && board[7] == 'X')
        cWhoWon = 'X';
    else if (board[2] == 'X' && board[5] == 'X' && board[8] == 'X')
        cWhoWon = 'X';
    else if (board[0] == 'X' && board[4] == 'X' && board[8] == 'X')
        cWhoWon = 'X';
    else if (board[2] == 'X' && board[4] == 'X' && board[6] == 'X')
        cWhoWon = 'X';
    else if (board[0] == 'O' && board[1] == 'O' && board[2] == 'O')
        cWhoWon = 'O';
    else if (board[3] == 'O' && board[4] == 'O' && board[5] == 'O')
        cWhoWon = 'O';
    else if (board[6] == 'O' && board[7] == 'O' && board[8] == 'O')
        cWhoWon = 'O';
    else if (board[0] == 'O' && board[3] == 'O' && board[6] == 'O')
        cWhoWon = 'O';
    else if (board[1] == 'O' && board[4] == 'O' && board[7] == 'O')
        cWhoWon = 'O';
    else if (board[2] == 'O' && board[5] == 'O' && board[8] == 'O')
        cWhoWon = 'O';
```

```
    else if (board[0] == 'O' && board[4] == 'O' && board[8] == 'O')
        cWhoWon = 'O';
    else if (board[2] == 'O' && board[4] == 'O' && board[6] == 'O')
        cWhoWon = 'O';
    if (cWhoWon == 'X') {
        printf("\nX Wins!\n");
        return;
    }
    if (cWhoWon == 'O') {
        printf("\nO Wins!\n");
        return;
    }
    //check for CAT / draw game
    for ( x = 0; x < 9; x++ ) {
        if ( board[x] != ' ')
        catTotal += 1;
    } //end for loop
    if ( catTotal == 9 ) {
        cWhoWon = 'C';
        printf("\nCAT Game!\n");
        return;
    } //end if
} //end function definition
```

Summary

- An array is a grouping of contiguous memory segments.
- Variables in an array share the same name.
- Variables in an array share the same data type.
- Individual variables in an array are called elements.
- Elements in an array are accessed with an index number.
- Assigning the single numeric value of 0 in an array declaration will, by default, assign all array elements the value of 0.
- Elements in a character array hold characters plus a special NULL termination character, which is represented by the character constant '\0'.
- When creating character arrays, be sure to allocate enough room to store the largest character sequence assignable. Also, remember to allow enough room in the character array for storing the NULL character ('\0').

- Use looping structures, such as the for loop, to iterate through each element in an array.

- When C encounters the break keyword in a loop, it moves program control to the next statement outside of the loop.

- C implements two-dimensional arrays as single-dimension arrays with pointers to other single-dimension arrays.

- The easiest way to understand or think about two-dimensional arrays is to visualize a table with rows and columns.

- Nested loops are necessary to search through a two-dimensional array.

Challenges

1. Build a program that uses a single-dimension array to store 10 numbers input by a user. After inputting the numbers, the user should see a menu with two options to sort and print the 10 numbers in ascending or descending order.

2. Create a student GPA average calculator. The program should prompt the user to enter up to 30 GPAs, which are stored in a single-dimension array. Each time the user enters a GPA, he should have the option to calculate the current GPA average or enter another GPA. Sample data for this program is shown here:

   GPA: 3.5

   GPA: 2.8

   GPA: 3.0

   GPA: 2.5

   GPA: 4.0

   GPA: 3.7

   GPA Average: 3.25

   Hint: Be careful not to calculate empty array elements into your student GPA average.

3. Create a program that allows a user to enter up to five names of friends. Use a two-dimensional array to store the friends' names. After each name is entered, the user should have the option to enter another name or print out a report that shows each name entered thus far.

4. Modify the Tic-Tac-Toe game to use a two-dimensional array instead of a single-dimension array.

5. Modify the Tic-Tac-Toe program or build your own Tic-Tac-Toe game to be a single-player game. (The user will play against the computer.)

7

Pointers

No doubt about it, pointers are one of the most challenging topics in C programming. Yet pointers are what make C one of the most robust languages in the computing industry for building programs unparalleled in efficiency and power.

There are many benefits of using pointers, such as faster program execution and the ability to access variables outside of the calling function.

Understanding pointers is of paramount importance to understanding the remainder of this book, and for that matter, the rest of what C has to offer. Despite pointers' challenges, keep one thing in mind: every beginning C programmer (including me) has struggled through pointer concepts. You can think of pointers as a rite of passage for any C programmer. To get started, I show you the following fundamentals:

- Pointer fundamentals
- Functions and pointers
- Passing arrays to functions
- The const qualifier
- Chapter program: Cryptogram

After mastering this chapter's concepts, you will be ready to study more sophisticated pointer concepts and their applications, such as strings, dynamic memory allocation, and various data structures.

Pointer Fundamentals

Pointers are powerful structures that can be used by C programmers to work with variables, functions, and data structures through their memory addresses. Pointers are a special type of variable that can contain a memory address as their value. In other words, a pointer variable contains a memory address that points to another variable. That may sound strange, so let's discuss an example.

Imagine that you have an integer variable called iResult that contains the value 75 and is located at memory address 0x948311. Now imagine that you have a pointer variable called myPointer, which instead of containing a regular data value contains the memory address 0x948311, the memory address of integer variable iResult. The memory address 0x948311 contains the value 75, which means that the pointer variable called myPointer indirectly points to the value of 75. This concept is known as *indirection*, and it is an essential pointer concept.

> **Hint**
>
> You may not have realized it at the time, but if you've completed Chapter 6, "Arrays," you've already worked with pointers. An array name is nothing more than a pointer to the start of the array.

Declaring and Initializing Pointer Variables

Pointer variables must be declared before they can be used, as shown in the following code:

```
int x = 0;
int iAge = 30;
int *ptrAge;
```

Simply place the indirection operator (*) in front of the variable name to declare a pointer. In the previous example, I declared three variables: two integer variables and one pointer variable. For readability, I use the naming convention ptr as a prefix. This helps me and other programmers identify this variable as a pointer.

> **Trick**
>
> While using a naming convention, such as ptr, is not technically required, doing so helps you identify the data type of the variable and, if possible, its purpose.

When I declared the pointer ptrAge, I was telling C that I want my pointer variable to indirectly point to an integer data type. My pointer variable, however, is not pointing to anything just yet.

To indirectly reference a value through a pointer, you must assign an address to the pointer, as shown here:

```
ptrAge = &iAge;
```

In this statement, I assign the memory address of the iAge variable to the pointer variable (ptrAge). Indirection in this case is accomplished by placing the unary operator (&) in front of the variable iAge. This statement is telling C that I want to assign the memory address of iAge to my pointer variable ptrAge.

The unary operator (&) is often referred to as the "address of" operator because, in this case, my pointer ptrAge is receiving the "address of" iAge.

Conversely, I can assign the contents of what my pointer variable points to—a nonpointer data value—as demonstrated next.

```
x = *ptrAge;
```

The variable x now contains the integer value of what ptrAge points to—in this case, the integer value 30.

To get a better idea of how pointers and indirection work, study Figure 7.1.

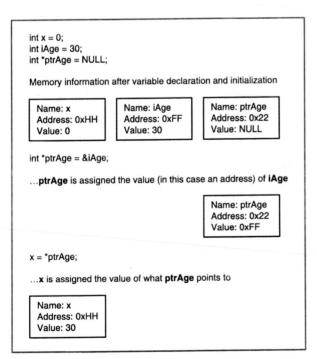

Figure 7.1
A graphical representation of indirection with pointers.

Not initializing your pointer variables can result in invalid data or invalid expression results. Pointer variables should always be initialized with another variable's memory address, with 0, or with the keyword NULL. The next code block demonstrates a few valid pointer initializations:

```
int *ptr1;
int *ptr2;
int *ptr3;
ptr1 = &x;
ptr2 = 0;
ptr3 = NULL;
```

Remembering that you can only assign pointer variables assigned memory addresses, 0, or the NULL value is the first step in learning to work with pointers. Consider the following example, in which I try to assign a nonaddress value to a pointer:

```
#include <stdio.h>

int main()
{
    int x = 5;
    int *iPtr;
    iPtr = 5; //this is wrong
    iPtr = x; //this is also wrong
    return 0;
}
```

You can see that I tried to assign the integer value 5 to my pointer. This type of assignment causes a compile-time error, as shown in Figure 7.2.

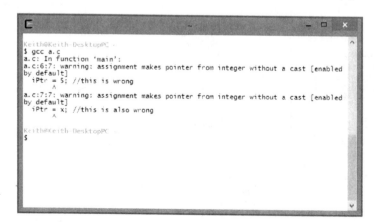

Figure 7.2
Assigning nonaddress values to pointers.

Trap

Assigning nonaddress values, such as numbers or characters, to a pointer without a cast results in compile-time errors.

You can, however, assign nonaddress values to pointers by using an indirection operator (*), as shown next:

```c
#include <stdio.h>

int main()
{
    int x = 5;
    int *iPtr;
    iPtr = &x; //iPtr is assigned the address of x
    *iPtr = 7; //the value of x is indirectly changed to 7
    return 0;
}
```

This program assigns the memory address of variable x to the pointer variable (iPtr) and then indirectly assigns the integer value 7 to variable x.

Printing Pointer Variable Contents

To verify indirection concepts, print the memory address of pointers and nonpointer variables using the %p conversion specifier. To demonstrate the %p conversion specifier, study the following program:

```c
#include <stdio.h>

int main()
{
    int x = 1;
    int *iPtr;
    iPtr = &x;
    *iPtr = 5;

    printf("\n*iPtr = %p\n&x = %p\n", iPtr, &x);
    return 0;
}
```

I use the %p conversion specifier to print the memory address for the pointer and integer variable. As shown in Figure 7.3, the pointer variable contains the same memory address (in hexadecimal format) of the integer variable x.

Figure 7.3
Printing a memory address with the %p conversion specifier.

The next program (and its output in Figure 7.4) continues to demonstrate indirection concepts and the %p conversion specifier:

```c
#include <stdio.h>

int main()
{
    int x = 5;
    int y = 10;
    int *iPtr = NULL;

    printf("\niPtr points to: %p\n", iPtr);

    //assign memory address of y to pointer
    iPtr = &y;
    printf("\niPtr now points to: %p\n", iPtr);

    //change the value of x to the value of y
    x = *iPtr;
    printf("\nThe value of x is now: %d\n", x);
```

```
    //change the value of y to 15
    *iPtr = 15;
    printf("\nThe value of y is now: %d\n", y);
    return 0;
}
```

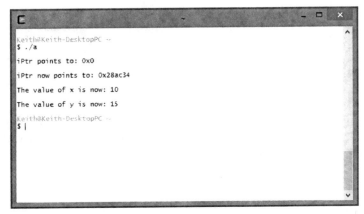

Figure 7.4
Using pointers and assignment statements to demonstrate indirection.

Functions and Pointers

One of the greatest benefits of using pointers is the ability to pass arguments to functions by reference. By default, arguments are passed by value in C, which involves making a copy of the incoming argument for the function to use. Depending on the storage requirements of the incoming argument, this may not be the most efficient use of memory. To demonstrate, study the following program:

```c
#include <stdio.h>

int addTwoNumbers(int, int);
int main()
{
    int x = 0;
    int y = 0; printf("\nEnter first number: ");
    scanf("%d", &x);
```

```
    printf("\nEnter second number: ");
    scanf("%d", &y);

    printf("\nResult is %d\n", addTwoNumbers(x, y));
    return 0;
} //end main

int addTwoNumbers(int x, int y)
{
    return x + y;
} //end addTwoNumbers
```

In this program, I pass two integer arguments to my addTwoNumbers function in a printf() function. This type of argument passing is called *passing by value*. More specifically, C reserves extra memory space to make a copy of variables x and y, and the copies of x and y are then sent to the function as arguments. But what does this mean? Two important concerns come to mind.

First, passing arguments by value is not the most efficient programming means for programming in C. Making copies of two integer variables may not seem like a lot of work, but in the real world, C programmers must strive to minimize memory use as much as possible. Think about embedded circuit design in which your memory resources are very limited. In these development situations, copying variables for arguments can make a big difference. Even if you are not programming embedded circuits, you can find performance degradation when passing large amounts of data by value. (Think of arrays or data structures that contain large amounts of information, such as employee data.)

Second, when C passes arguments by value, you are unable to modify the original contents of the incoming parameters. This is because C has made a copy of the original variable, so only the copy is modified. This can be a good thing and a bad thing. For example, you may not want the receiving function modifying the variable's original contents and, in this case, passing arguments by value is preferred. Moreover, passing arguments by value is one way programmers can implement information hiding as discussed in Chapter 5, "Structured Programming."

To further demonstrate the concepts of passing arguments by value, study the following program and its output shown in Figure 7.5:

```
#include <stdio.h>
void demoPassByValue(int);

int main()
{
    int x = 0;
```

```
    printf("\nEnter a number: ");
    scanf("%d", &x);

    demoPassByValue(x);

    printf("\nThe original value of x did not change: %d\n", x);
    return 0;
} //end main

void demoPassByValue(int x)
{
    x += 5;
    printf("\nThe value of x is: %d\n", x);
} //end demoPassByValue
```

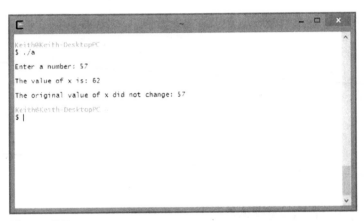

Figure 7.5
Implementing information hiding by passing arguments by value.

After studying the code, you can see that I attempt to modify the incoming parameter by incrementing it by five. The argument appears to be modified when I print the contents in the demoPassByValue's printf() function. However, when I print the contents of variable x from the main() function, you can see that x indeed was not modified.

To solve this problem, you use pointers to pass arguments *by reference*. More specifically, you can pass the address of the variable (argument) to the function using indirection, as demonstrated in the next program and in Figure 7.6:

```c
#include <stdio.h>
void demoPassByReference(int *);

int main()
{
    int x = 0;

    printf("\nEnter a number: ");
    scanf("%d", &x);

    demoPassByReference(&x);

    printf("\nThe original value of x is: %d\n", x);
    return 0;
} //end main

void demoPassByReference(int *ptrX)
{
    *ptrX += 5;
    printf("\nThe value of x is now: %d\n", *ptrX);
} //end demoPassByReference
```

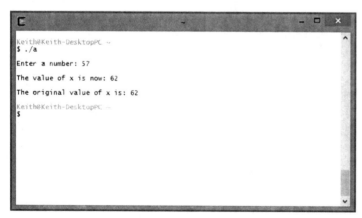

Figure 7.6

Passing an argument by reference using indirection.

To pass arguments by reference, you need to be aware of a few subtle differences in the preceding program. The first noticeable difference is in the function prototype, as shown next:

```
void demoPassByReference(int *);
```

I tell C that my function takes a pointer as an argument by placing the indirection (*) operator after the data type. The next slight difference is in my function call, to which I pass the memory address of the variable x by placing the unary (&) operator in front of the variable:

```
demoPassByReference(&x);
```

The rest of the pertinent indirection activities are performed in the function implementation, where I tell the function header to expect an incoming parameter (pointer) that points to an integer value. This is known as *passing by reference*!

```
void demoPassByReference(int *ptrX)
```

To modify the original contents of the argument, I must again use the indirection operator (*), which tells C that I want to access the contents of the memory location contained in the pointer variable. Specifically, I increment the original variable contents by five:

```
*ptrX += 5;
```

I use the indirection operator in a printf() function to print the pointer's contents:

```
printf("\nThe value of x is now: %d\n", *ptrX);
```

Trap

If you forget to place the indirection (*) operator in front of a pointer in a print statement that displays a number with the %d conversion specifier, C prints a numeric representation of the pointer address:

```
printf("\nThe value of x is now: %d\n", ptrX); //this is wrong
printf("\nThe value of x is now: %d\n", *ptrX); //this is right
```

Up until now, you may have been wondering why it is necessary to place an ampersand (also known as the "address of" operator) in front of variables in scanf() functions. Quite simply, the address operator provides the scanf() function the memory address to which C should write data that the user types.

Passing Arrays to Functions

You may remember from Chapter 6 that arrays are groupings of contiguous memory segments and that the array name itself is a pointer to the first memory location in the contiguous memory segment. Arrays and pointers are closely related in C. In fact, passing an array name to a pointer assigns the first memory location of the array to the pointer variable. To demonstrate this concept, the next program creates and initializes an array of five elements and declares a pointer that is initialized to the array name. Initializing a pointer to an array name stores the first address of the array in the pointer, which is shown in Figure 7.7.

After initializing the pointer, I can access the first memory address of the array and the array's first element:

```
#include <stdio.h>

int main()
{
    int iArray[5] = {1,2,3,4,5};
    int *iPtr = iArray;

    printf("\nAddress of pointer: %p\n", iPtr);
    printf("First address of array: %p\n", &iArray[0]);
    printf("\nPointer points to: %d\n", *iPtr);
    printf("First element of array contains: %d\n", iArray[0]);
    return 0;
}
```

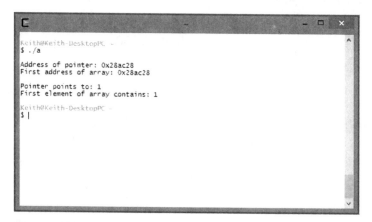

Figure 7.7
Assigning the first address of an array to a pointer.

Knowing that an array name contains a memory address that points to the first element in the array, you can surmise that array names can be treated much like a pointer when passing arrays to functions. It is not necessary to deal with unary (&) or indirection (*) operators when passing arrays to functions, however. More importantly, arrays passed as arguments are passed by reference automatically. That's an important concept, so I'll state it again. *Arrays passed as arguments are passed by reference.*

To pass an array to a function, you need to define your function prototype and definition so that they expect to receive an array as an argument. The next program and its output in Figure 7.8 demonstrate this concept by passing a character array to a function that calculates the length of the incoming string (character array):

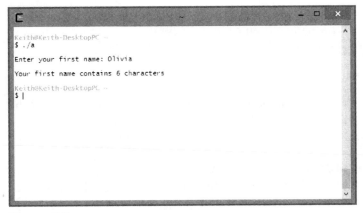

Figure 7.8
Passing an array as an argument.

```c
#include <stdio.h>
int nameLength(char []);

int main()
{
    char aName[20] = {'\0'};

    printf("\nEnter your first name: ");
    scanf("%s", aName);

    printf("\nYour first name contains ");
    printf("%d characters\n", nameLength(aName));
    return 0;
} //end main
```

```
int nameLength(char name[])
{
    int x = 0;
    while ( name[x] != '\0' )
        x++;
    return x;
} //end nameLength
```

You can build your function prototype to receive an array as an argument by placing empty brackets in the argument list as shown:

```
int nameLength(char []);
```

This function prototype tells C to expect an array as an argument. More specifically, the function will receive the first memory address in the array. When calling the function, I need only to pass the array name, as shown in the next print statement:

```
printf("%d characters\n", nameLength(aName));
```

Also notice in the preceding program that I did not use the address of (&) operator in front of the array name in the scanf() function. This is because an array name in C already contains a memory address, which is the address of the first element in the array.

This program is a good demonstration of passing arrays as arguments, but it doesn't serve well to prove that arrays are passed by reference. To do so, study the following program and its output in Figure 7.9, which modifies array contents using pass by reference techniques:

```
#include <stdio.h>
void squareNumbers(int []);

int main()
{
    int x;
    int iNumbers[3] = {2, 4, 6};

    printf("\nThe current array values are: ");
    for ( x = 0; x < 3; x++ )
        printf("%d ", iNumbers[x]); //print contents of array
    printf("\n");

    squareNumbers(iNumbers);
```

```
    printf("\nThe modified array values are: ");
    for ( x = 0; x < 3; x++ )
    printf("%d ", iNumbers[x]); //print modified array contents printf("\n");
    return 0;
} //end main

void squareNumbers(int num[])
{
    int x;
    for ( x = 0; x < 3; x++ )
        num[x] = num[x] * num[x]; //modify the array contents
} //end squareNumbers
```

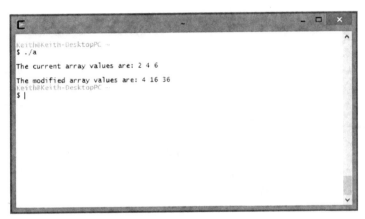

Figure 7.9
Modifying array contents through indirection and passing arrays to functions.

The const Qualifier

You are now aware that arguments can be passed to functions in one of two ways: pass by value and pass by reference. When passing arguments by value, C makes a copy of the argument for the receiving function to use. Also known as *information hiding*, this prevents the direct changing of the incoming argument's contents, but it creates additional overhead when passing large structures to functions. Passing arguments by reference, however, enables C programmers to modify argument contents via pointers.

There are times, however, when you want the power and speed of passing arguments by reference without the security risk of changing a variable's (argument's) contents. C programmers can accomplish this with the const qualifier.

You may remember from Chapter 2, "Primary Data Types," that the const qualifier allows you to create read-only variables. You can also use the const qualifier in conjunction with pointers to achieve a read-only argument while still achieving the pass by reference capability. To demonstrate, the next program passes a read-only integer type argument to a function:

```c
#include <stdio.h>
void printArgument(const int *);

int main()
{
    int iNumber = 5;

    printArgument(&iNumber); //pass read-only argument
    return 0;
} //end main

void printArgument(const int *num) //pass by reference, but read-only
{
    printf("\nRead Only Argument is: %d ", *num);
}
```

Remembering that arrays are passed to functions by reference, you should know that function implementations can alter the original array's contents. To prevent an array argument from being altered in a function, use the const qualifier, as demonstrated in the next program:

```c
#include <stdio.h>
void printArray(const int []);

int main()
{
    int iNumbers[3] = {2, 4, 6};

    printArray(iNumbers);
    return 0;
} //end main
```

```
void printArray(const int num[]) //pass by reference, but read-only
{
    int x;
    printf("\nArray contents are: ");
    for ( x = 0; x < 3; x++ )
        printf("%d ", num[x]);
}
```

As shown in the preceding program, you can pass an array to a function as read-only by using the const qualifier. To do so, you must tell the function prototype and function definition that it should expect a read-only argument by using the const keyword.

To prove the read-only concept, consider the next program, which attempts to modify the read-only argument in an assignment statement from within the function:

```
#include <stdio.h>
void modifyArray(const int []);

int main()
{
    int iNumbers[3] = {2, 4, 6};

    modifyArray(iNumbers);

    return 0;
} //end main

void modifyArray(const int num[])
{
    int x;
    for ( x = 0; x < 3; x++ )
    num[x] = num[x] * num[x]; //this will not work!
}
```

Notice the output in Figure 7.10. The C compiler warns me with an error that I'm attempting to modify a read-only location.

In summary, the const qualifier is a nice solution for securing argument contents in a pass by reference environment.

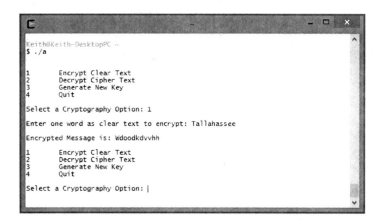

Figure 7.10
Triggering a compiler error by attempting to modify a read-only memory location.

Chapter Program: Cryptogram

As revealed in Figure 7.11, the chapter-based program Cryptogram uses many of the techniques you have learned thus far about pointers, arrays, and functions. Before you proceed directly to the program code, however, the next section gives you some basic information on cryptograms and encryption to assist you in understanding the chapter-based program's intent and application.

Figure 7.11
The chapter-based program, Cryptogram, passes arrays to functions to encrypt and decrypt a word.

Introduction to Encryption

Encryption is a subset of technologies and sciences under the cryptography umbrella. Like the world of computer programming, cryptography and encryption have many specialized keywords, definitions, and techniques. It is prudent to list some of the more common definitions in this section before continuing:

- **Cryptography**—The art and science of protecting or obscuring messages.
- **Cipher text**—A message obscured by applying an encryption algorithm.
- **Clear text**—Plain text or a message readable by humans.
- **Cryptogram**—An encrypted or protected message.
- **Cryptographer**—A person or specialist who practices encrypting or protecting messages.
- **Encryption**—The process by which clear text is converted into cipher text.
- **Decryption**—The process of converting cipher text into clear text; generally involves knowing a key or formula.
- **Key**—The formula used to decrypt an encrypted message.

Encryption techniques have been applied for hundreds of years, although it wasn't until the advent of the Internet and the computer age that encryption gained a level of unprecedented public attention.

Whether it's protecting your credit card information with dot-com purchases or keeping your personal data on your home PC safe and secure, computing provides a new level of anxiety for everyone.

Fortunately, there are a number of good guys out there trying to figure out the right mixture of computer science, math, and cryptography to build safe systems for private and sensitive data. These good guys are generally computer companies and computing professionals who attempt to alleviate anxiety through the promise of intangible or at least unreadable data using encryption.

In a simplified manner, encryption uses many techniques for converting human-readable messages, known as clear text, into an unreadable or obscure message called *cipher text*. Encrypted messages are generally locked and unlocked with the same key or algorithm. Keys used to lock and unlock secured messages, or *cryptograms*, can either be stored in the encrypted message itself or be used in conjunction with outside sources, such as account numbers and passwords.

The first step in encrypting any message is to create an encryption algorithm. An oversimplified encryption algorithm discussed in this section is the technique or algorithm called *shift by n*, which changes the shape or meaning of a message. The shift by n algorithm basically says to move each character up or down a scale by a certain number of increments. For example, I can encrypt the following message by shifting each character by two letters:

```
Meet me at seven
```

Shifting each character by two letters produces the following result:

```
Oggv og cv ugxgp
```

The key in the shift by n algorithm is the number used in shifting (the *n* in shift by n). Without this key, it is difficult to decipher or decrypt the encrypted message. It's really quite simple! Of course, this is not an encryption algorithm that the CIA would use to pass data to and from its agents, but you get the point.

The encryption algorithm is only as good as its key is safe. To demonstrate, consider that your house is locked and safe until an unauthorized person gains physical access to your key. Even though you have the best locks money can buy, they no longer provide security because an unwanted person has the key to unlock your house.

As you will see in the next section, you can build your own simple encryption processes with encryption algorithms and encryption keys using C, the ASCII character set, and the shift by n algorithm.

Building the Cryptogram Program

Using your knowledge of beginning encryption concepts, you can easily build an encryption program in C that uses the shift by n algorithm to generate a key and encrypt and decrypt a message.

As shown in Figure 7.11, the user is presented with an option to encrypt a message, decrypt a message, or generate a new key. When a new key is generated, the encryption algorithm uses the new key to shift each letter of the message by *n*, which is the random number generated by selecting the Generate New Key option. The same key is again used to decrypt the message.

If you generate a new key after encrypting a message, it is quite possible that you will be unable to decrypt the previously encrypted message. This demonstrates the importance of knowing the encryption key on both ends of the cryptogram.

All the code needed to build the Cryptogram program is shown next:

```
#include <stdio.h>
#include <stdlib.h>
#include <time.h>

//function prototypes
void encrypt(char [], int);
void decrypt(char [], int);

int main()
{
    char myString[21] = {0};
    int iSelection = 0;
    int iRand;
    srand(time(NULL));
    iRand = (rand() % 4) + 1; // random #, 1-4
```

```
    while ( iSelection != 4 ) {
        printf("\n\n1\tEncrypt Clear Text\n");
        printf("2\tDecrypt Cipher Text\n");
        printf("3\tGenerate New Key\n");
        printf("4\tQuit\n");
        printf("\nSelect a Cryptography Option: ");
        scanf("%d", &iSelection);
        switch (iSelection) {
        case 1:
            printf("\nEnter one word as clear text to encrypt: ");
            scanf("%s", myString);
            encrypt(myString, iRand);
            break;
        case 2:
            printf("\nEnter cipher text to decrypt: ");
            scanf("%s", myString);
            decrypt(myString, iRand);
            break;
        case 3:
            iRand = (rand() % 4) + 1; // random #, 1-4
            printf("\nNew Key Generated\n");
            break;
        } //end switch
    } //end loop
    return 0;
} //end main

void encrypt(char sMessage[], int random)
{
    int x = 0;
//encrypt the message by shifting each character's ASCII value
    while ( sMessage[x] ) {
        sMessage[x] += random;
        x++;
    } //end loop
    x = 0;
    printf("\nEncrypted Message is: ");
```

```
//print the encrypted message
    while ( sMessage[x] ) {
        printf("%c", sMessage[x]);
        x++;
    } //end loop
} //end encrypt function
void decrypt(char sMessage[], int random)
{
    int x = 0; x = 0;

//decrypt the message by shifting each character's ASCII value
    while ( sMessage[x] ) {
        sMessage[x] = sMessage[x] - random;
        x++;
    } //end loop
    x = 0;
    printf("\nDecrypted Message is: ");

//print the decrypted message
    while ( sMessage[x] ) {
        printf("%c", sMessage[x]);
        x++;
    } //end loop
} //end decrypt function
```

Summary

- Pointers are special variables that contain a memory address pointing to another variable.
- Place the indirection operator (*) in front of the variable name to declare a pointer.
- The unary operator (&) is often referred to as the address of operator.
- Always initialize pointer variables with another variable's memory address, with 0, or with the keyword NULL.
- You can print the memory address of pointers using the %p conversion specifier.
- By default, arguments are passed by value in C, which involves making a copy of the incoming argument for the function to use.
- You can use pointers to pass arguments by reference.

- Passing an array name to a pointer assigns the first memory location of the array to the pointer variable. Similarly, initializing a pointer to an array name stores the first address of the array in the pointer.
- You can use the const qualifier in conjunction with pointers to achieve a read-only argument while still achieving the pass by reference capability.

Challenges

1. Build a program that performs the following operations:

   - Declares three pointer variables called iPtr of type int, cPtr of type char, and fFloat of type float
   - Declares three new variables called iNumber of int type, fNumber of float type, and cCharacter of char type
   - Assigns the address of each nonpointer variable to the matching pointer variable
   - Prints the value of each nonpointer variable
   - Prints the value of each pointer variable
   - Prints the address of each nonpointer variable
   - Prints the address of each pointer variable

2. Create a program that allows a user to select one of the following four menu options:

   - Enter New Integer Value
   - Print Pointer Address
   - Print Integer Address
   - Print Integer Value

   For this program, you need to create two variables: one integer data type and one pointer. Using indirection, assign any new integer value that the user enters through an appropriate pointer.

3. Create a dice rolling game. The game should allow a user to toss up to six dice at a time. Each toss of a die will be stored in a six-element integer array. The array is created in the main() function but passed to a new function called TossDie(). The TossDie() function will take care of generating random numbers from one to six and assigning them to the appropriate array element number.

4. Modify the Cryptogram program to use a different type of key system or algorithm. Consider using a user-defined key or a different character set.

Strings

Strings use many concepts that you have already learned about in this book, such as functions, arrays, and pointers. This chapter shows you how to build and use strings in your C programs while also outlining the intimate relationships strings have with pointers and arrays. It also covers many new common library functions for manipulating, converting, and searching strings, as well as the following:

- Introduction to strings
- Reading and printing strings
- String arrays
- Converting strings to numbers
- Manipulating strings
- Analyzing strings
- Chapter program: Word Find

Introduction to Strings

Strings are groupings of letters, numbers, and many other characters. C programmers can create and initialize a string using a character array and a terminating NULL character, as shown next:

```
char myString[5] = {'M', 'i', 'k', 'e', '\0'};
```

Figure 8.1 depicts this declared array of characters.

Trap

When creating character arrays, it is important to allocate enough room for the NULL character because many C library functions look for the NULL character when processing character arrays. If the NULL character is not found, some C library functions may not produce the desired result.

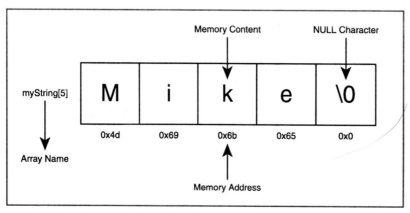

Figure 8.1
Depicting an array of characters.

You can also create and initialize the variable myString with a string literal. *String literals* are groupings of characters enclosed in quotation marks, as shown next:

```
char myString[] = "Mike";
```

Assigning a string literal to a character array, as the preceding code shows, creates the necessary number of memory elements—in this case, five including the NULL character.

You know that strings are arrays of characters in a logical sense, but it's just as important to know that strings are implemented as a pointer to a segment of memory. More specifically, string names are really just pointers to the first character's memory address in a string.

To demonstrate this thought, consider the following program statement:

```
char *myString = "Mike";
```

This statement declares a pointer variable and assigns the string literal "Mike" to the first and subsequent memory locations that the pointer variable myString points to. In other words, the pointer variable myString points to the first character in the string "Mike".

To further demonstrate this concept, study the following program and its output in Figure 8.2, which reveals how you can reference strings through pointers and traverse them similar to arrays:

```
#include <stdio.h>

int main()
{
    char *myString = "Mike";
    int x;

    printf("\nThe pointer variable's value is: %p\n", *myString);
    printf("\nThe pointer variable points to: %s\n", myString);
    printf("\nThe memory locations for each character are: \n\n");

    //access & print each memory address in hexadecimal format
    for ( x = 0; x < 5; x++ )
        printf("%p\n", myString[x]);
    return 0;
} //end main
```

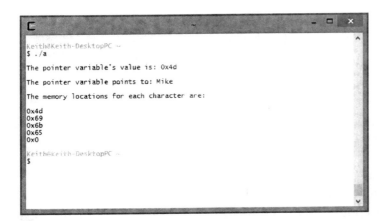

Figure 8.2
Creating, manipulating, and printing strings with pointers and arrays of characters.

ARE STRINGS DATA TYPES?

The concept of a string is sometimes taken for granted in high-level languages such as Visual Basic. This is because many high-level languages implement strings as a data type, just like an integer or double. In fact, you may be thinking—or at least hoping—that C contains a string data type as shown next:

```
str myString = "Mike"; //not possible, no such data type
string myString = "Mike"; //not possible, no such data type
```

C does not identify strings as a data type; rather, C strings are simply character arrays.

Figure 8.3 further depicts the notion of strings as pointers.

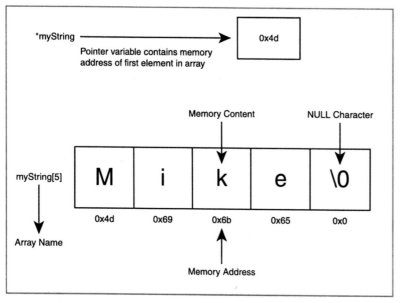

Figure 8.3
Using pointers, memory addresses, and characters to demonstrate how strings are assembled.

After studying the preceding program and Figure 8.3, you can see how the pointer variable myString contains the value of a memory address (printed in hexadecimal format) that points to the first character in the string "Mike", followed by subsequent characters and finally the NULL zero to indicate the end of the string.

In the next few sections, you continue your investigation into strings and their use by learning how to handle string I/O and how to convert, manipulate, and search strings using a few old and new C libraries and their associated functions.

Reading and Printing Strings

Chapter 6, "Arrays," provided you with an overview of how to read and print array contents. To read and print a character array, use the %s conversion specifier, as demonstrated in the next program:

```c
#include <stdio.h>

int main()
{
    char color[12] = {'\0'};

    printf("Enter your favorite color: ");
    scanf("%s", color);
    printf("\nYou entered: %s", color);
    return 0;
} //end main
```

The preceding program demonstrates reading a string into a character array with initialized and allocated memory (char color[12] = {'\0'};), but what about reading strings from standard input for which you do not know the string length? Many C texts overlook this. It might be natural to assume that you can use the standard library's scanf() function, as demonstrated next, to capture and assign string data from standard input to a variable:

```c
#include <stdio.h>

int main()
{
    char *color;

    printf("\nEnter your favorite color: ");
    scanf("%s", color); //this will NOT work!
    printf("\nYou entered: %s", color);
    return 0;
} //end main
```

Unfortunately, this program may not work; it will compile, but because scanf() writes to an undefined area of memory, execution of the program may work one time and another time result in a segmentation fault, even if the operating system prevents a crash.

This problem occurs because not only must you declare a string as a pointer to a character, but you must also allocate memory for it. Remember that when it's first created, a string is nothing more than a pointer that points to nothing valid. Moreover, when the scanf() function attempts to assign data to the pointer's location, the program may not work correctly because memory has not been properly allocated.

For now, you should simply use initialized character arrays with sufficient memory allocated to read strings from standard input. In Chapter 10, "Dynamic Memory Allocation," I discuss the secret to assigning data from standard input to strings (pointer variables).

String Arrays

Now you know that strings are pointers and, in an abstract sense, strings are arrays of characters. So, if you need an array of strings, do you need a two-dimensional array or a single-dimension array? The correct answer is both. You can create an array of strings with a one-dimensional pointer array and assign string literals to it, or you can create a two-dimensional pointer array, allowing C to reserve enough memory for each character array.

To demonstrate how an array of strings can be created using a single-dimension pointer array of type char, study the following program and its output shown in Figure 8.4:

```
#include <stdio.h>

int main()
{
    char *strNames[5] = {0};
    char answer[80] = {0};
    int x;
    strNames[0] = "Michael";
    strNames[1] = "Sheila";
    strNames[2] = "Spencer";
    strNames[3] = "Hunter";
    strNames[4] = "Kenya";

    printf("\nNames in pointer array of type char:\n\n");
```

```
    for ( x = 0; x < 5; x++ )
        printf("%s\n", strNames[x]);
    return 0;
} //end main
```

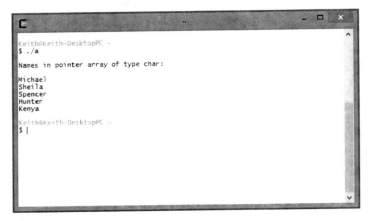

Figure 8.4
Printing strings with a character pointer array.

In the preceding program, it is important to note that this array of strings is really an array of character pointers. C is able to treat each element in the array as a string because I used string literals, which C places in protected memory.

Another way to simulate an array of strings is to use a two-dimensional pointer array of type char, as seen in the next program:

```
#include <stdio.h>

int main()
{
    char *colors[3][10] = {'\0'};

    printf("\nEnter 3 colors separated by spaces: ");
    scanf("%s %s %s", colors[0], colors[1], colors[2]);

    printf("\nYou entered: ");
    printf("%s %s %s\n", colors[0], colors[1], colors[2]);
    return 0;
}
```

In the preceding program, I declared a 3×10 (three by ten) two-dimensional character array that reserves enough memory for 30 characters. Notice that I only need to tell C to reference the first dimension of each element in the character array when referencing a single string. Providing I've allocated enough elements in the second dimension, I can easily use scanf() to grab text that the user entered. In Chapter 10, I show you how to grab portions of contiguous memory without first allocating it in an array.

Converting Strings to Numbers

When dealing with ASCII characters, how do you differentiate between numbers and letters? The answer is twofold. First, programmers assign like characters to various data types, such as characters (char) and integers (int), to differentiate between numbers and letters. This is a straightforward and well-understood approach for differentiating between data types. But there are less defined occasions when programmers need to convert data from one type to another. For example, sometimes you want to convert a string to a number.

Fortunately, the C standard library stdlib.h provides a few functions that convert strings to numbers. Here are two of the most common string conversion functions:

- atof—Converts a string to a floating-point number
- atoi—Converts a string to an integer

Both of these functions are demonstrated in the next program, and the output is shown in Figure 8.5:

```
#include <stdio.h>
#include <stdlib.h>

int main()
{
    char *str1 = "123.79";
    char *str2 = "55";
    float x;
    int y;

    printf("\nString 1 is \"%s\"\n", str1);
    printf("String 2 is \"%s\"\n", str2);

    x = atof(str1);
    y = atoi(str2);
```

```
    printf("\nString 1 converted to a float is %.2f\n", x);
    printf("String 2 converted to an integer is %d\n", y);
    return 0;
} //end main
```

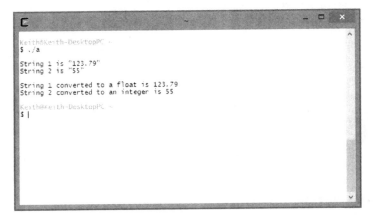

Figure 8.5
Converting string literals to numeric types float and int.

Trick

When printed to standard output, strings are not surrounded by quotes automatically, as depicted in Figure 8.5. Should you want to explicitly print quotation marks, you can do so by using a conversion specifier, more specifically the \" conversion specifier, in a printf() function as shown here:

```
    printf("\nString 1 is \"%s\"\n", str1);
```

You may be wondering why string conversion is so important. Well, attempting numeric arithmetic on strings can produce unexpected results, as demonstrated in the next program and in Figure 8.6:

```
#include <stdio.h>

int main()
{
    char *str1 = "37";
    char *str2 = "20";
```

```
        //produces invalid results
        printf("\nString 1 + String 2 is %d\n", *str1 + *str2);
        return 0;
} //end main
```

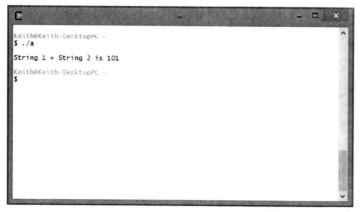

Figure 8.6
Invalid arithmetic results generated by not converting strings to numbers.

In the preceding code, I tried to convert the result using the %d conversion specifier. (%d is the decimal integer conversion specifier.) This is not enough, however, to convert strings or character arrays to numbers, as demonstrated in Figure 8.6.

To correct this problem, you can use string conversion functions, as demonstrated in the next program and its output in Figure 8.7.

```
#include <stdio.h>

int main()
{
    char *str1 = "37";
    char *str2 = "20";
    int iResult;

    iResult = atoi(str1) + atoi(str2);

    printf("\nString 1 + String 2 is %d\n", iResult);
    return 0;
} //end main
```

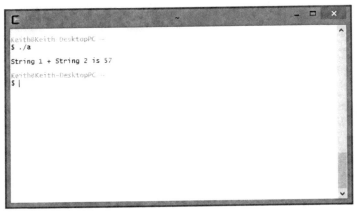

Figure 8.7
Using the atoi function to convert strings to numbers.

Manipulating Strings

A common practice among programmers is manipulating string data, such as copying one string into another and concatenating (gluing) strings to each other. Also common is the need to convert strings to either all lowercase or all uppercase, which can be important when comparing one string to another. I show you how to perform these string manipulations in the following sections.

The strlen() Function

The string length (strlen()) function is part of the string-handling library <string.h> and is quite simple to understand and use. strlen() takes a reference to a string and returns the numeric string length up to the NULL or terminating character, but not including the NULL character.

The next program and Figure 8.8 demonstrate the strlen() function:

```c
#include <stdio.h>
#include <string.h>

int main()
{
    char *str1 = "Michael";
    char str2[] = "Vine";

    printf("\nThe length of string 1 is %d\n", strlen(str1));
    printf("The length of string 2 is %d\n", strlen(str2));
    return 0;
} // end main
```

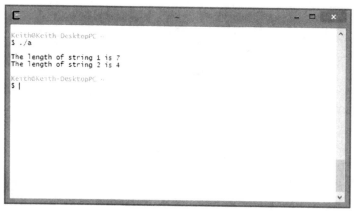

Figure 8.8
Using the strlen() function to determine the length of strings.

The tolower() and toupper() Functions

An important reason for converting strings to either all uppercase or all lowercase is for string comparisons.

The character-handling library <ctype.h> provides many character manipulation functions such as tolower() and toupper(). These functions provide an easy way to convert a single character to either uppercase or lowercase. (Notice I said single character.) To convert an entire character array to either all uppercase or all lowercase, you need to work a little harder.

One solution is to build your own user-defined functions for converting character arrays to uppercase or lowercase by looping through each character in the string and using the strlen() function to determine when to stop looping and converting each character to either lower- or uppercase with tolower() and toupper(). This solution is demonstrated in the next program, which uses two user-defined functions and, of course, the character-handling functions tolower() and toupper() to convert my first name to all lowercase and my last name to all uppercase. The output is shown in Figure 8.9:

```
#include <stdio.h>
#include <ctype.h>
#include <string.h>

//function prototypes
void convertL(char *);
void convertU(char *);

int main()
{
```

```
        char name1[] = "Michael";
        char name2[] = "Vine";

        convertL(name1);
        convertU(name2);
        return 0;
} //end main

void convertL(char *str)
{
    int x;
        for ( x = 0; x <= strlen(str); x++ ) str[x] = tolower(str[x]);
            printf("\nFirst name converted to lower case is %s\n", str);
} // end convertL

void convertU(char *str)
{
    int x;
    for ( x = 0; x <= strlen(str); x++ )
        str[x] = toupper(str[x]);
    printf("Last name converted to upper case is %s\n", str);
} // end convertU
```

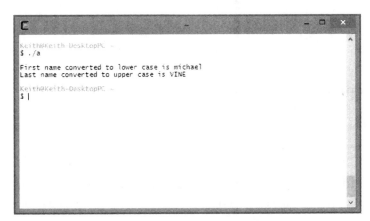

Figure 8.9
Manipulating character arrays with functions tolower() and toupper().

The strcpy() Function

The strcpy() function copies the contents of one string into another string. As you might imagine, it takes two arguments and is pretty straightforward to use, as the next program and Figure 8.10 demonstrate:

```c
#include <stdio.h>
#include <string.h>

int main()
{
    char str1[11];
    char *str2 = "C Language";

    printf("\nString 1 now contains %s\n", strcpy(str1, str2));
    return 0;
} // end main
```

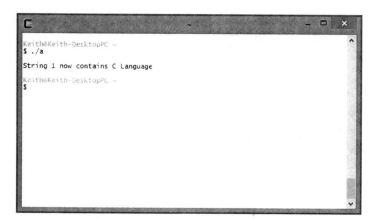

Figure 8.10
The output of copying one string to another using the strcpy() function.

The strcpy() function takes two strings as arguments. The first argument is the string to be copied into, and the second argument is the string that will be copied from. After copying string 2 (second argument) into string 1 (first argument), the strcpy() function returns the value of string 1.

Note that I declared string 1 (str1) as a character array rather than as a pointer to a char type. Moreover, I gave the character array 11 elements to handle the number characters plus a NULL character. You cannot assign data to an empty string without first allocating memory to it. I'll discuss this more in Chapter 10.

The strcat() Function

Another interesting and sometimes useful string library function is strcat(), which concatenates or glues one string to another.

> **Hint**
>
> To *concatenate* is to glue one or more pieces of data together or to connect one or more links.

Like the strcpy() function, the strcat() function takes two string arguments, as the next program demonstrates:

```c
#include <stdio.h>
#include <string.h>

int main()
{
    char str1[40] = "Computer Science ";
    char str2[] = "is applied mathematics";

    printf("\n%s\n", strcat(str1, str2));
    return 0;
} // end main
```

As Figure 8.11 demonstrates, the second string argument (str2) is concatenated to the first string argument (str1). After concatenating the two strings, the strcat() function returns the value in str1. Note that I had to include an extra space at the end of str1 "Computer Science" because the strcat() function does not add a space between the two merged strings.

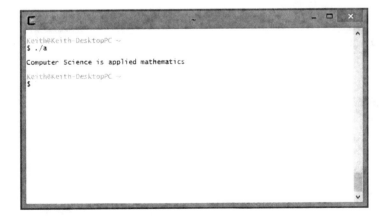

Figure 8.11
Using the strcat() function to glue strings together.

Analyzing Strings

In the next couple of sections, I discuss a few more functions of the string-handling library that enable you to perform various analyses of strings. More specifically, you learn how to compare two strings for equality and search strings for the occurrence of characters.

The strcmp() Function

strcmp() is an interesting and useful function that is primarily used to compare two strings for equality. Comparing strings is actually a common process for computer and noncomputer uses. To demonstrate, consider an old library card-catalog system that used human labor to manually sort book references by various keys (author name, ISBN, title, and so on). Most modern libraries now rely on computer systems and software to automate the process of sorting data for the card catalog system. Keep in mind that the computer does not know that letter A is greater than letter B, or better yet, that the exclamation mark (!) is less than the letter A. To differentiate between characters, computer systems rely on character codes such as the ASCII character-coding system.

Using character-coding systems, programmers can build sorting software that compares strings (characters). Moreover, C programmers can use built-in string-handling functions, such as strcmp(), to accomplish the same. To prove this, study the following program and its output shown in Figure 8.12:

```
#include <stdio.h>
#include <string.h>

int main()
{
    char *str1 = "A";
    char *str2 = "A";
    char *str3 = "!";

    printf("\nstr1 = %s\n", str1);
    printf("\nstr2 = %s\n", str2);
    printf("\nstr3 = %s\n", str3);
    printf("\nstrcmp(str1, str2) = %d\n", strcmp(str1, str2));
    printf("\nstrcmp(str1, str3) = %d\n", strcmp(str1, str3));
    printf("\nstrcmp(str3, str1) = %d\n", strcmp(str3, str1));

    if ( strcmp(str1, str2) == 0 )
        printf("\nLetter A is equal to letter A\n");
```

```
    if ( strcmp(str1, str3) > 0 )
        printf("Letter A is greater than character !\n");
    if ( strcmp(str3, str1) < 0 )
        printf("Character ! is less than letter A\n");
    return 0;
} // end main
```

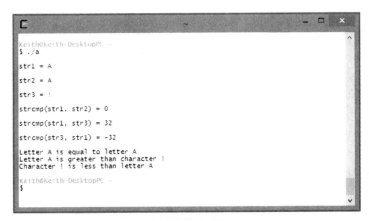

```
Keith@Keith-DesktopPC ~
$ ./a
str1 = A
str2 = A
str3 = !
strcmp(str1, str2) = 0
strcmp(str1, str3) = 32
strcmp(str3, str1) = -32
Letter A is equal to letter A
Letter A is greater than character !
Character ! is less than letter A
Keith@Keith-DesktopPC ~
$
```

Figure 8.12
Comparing strings using the strcmp() function.

The strcmp() function takes two strings as arguments and compares them using corresponding character codes. After comparing the two strings, the strcmp() function returns a single numeric value that indicates whether the first string is equal to, less than, or greater than the second string. Table 8.1 describes the strcmp() function's return values in further detail.

TABLE 8.1 RETURN VALUES AND DESCRIPTIONS FOR THE STRCMP() FUNCTION

Sample Function	Return Value	Description
strcmp(string1, string2)	0	string1 is equal to string2
strcmp(string1, string2)	<0	string1 is less than string2
strcmp(string1, string2)	>0	string1 is greater than string2

The strstr() Function

strstr() is a useful function for analyzing two strings. More specifically, the strstr() function takes two strings as arguments and searches the first string for an occurrence of the second. This type of search capability is demonstrated in the next program, and its output is shown in Figure 8.13:

```c
#include <stdio.h>
#include <string.h>

int main()
{
    char *str1 = "Analyzing strings with the strstr() function";
    char *str2 = "ing";
    char *str3 = "xyz";

    printf("\nstr1 = %s\n", str1);
    printf("\nstr2 = %s\n", str2);
    printf("\nstr3 = %s\n", str3);

    if ( strstr(str1, str2) != NULL )
        printf("\nstr2 was found in str1\n");
    else
        printf("\nstr2 was not found in str1\n");

    if ( strstr(str1, str3) != NULL )
        printf("\nstr3 was found in str1\n");
    else
        printf("\nstr3 was not found in str1\n");
    return 0;
} // end main
```

As you can see from the preceding program, the strstr() function takes two strings as arguments. The strstr() function looks for the first occurrence of the second argument in the first argument. If the string in the second argument is found in the string in the first argument, the strstr() function returns a pointer to the string in the first argument. Otherwise, it returns NULL.

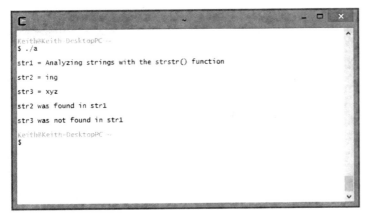

Figure 8.13
Using the strstr() function to search one string for another.

Chapter Program: Word Find

Word Find is a straightforward program that uses strings and many other chapter-based concepts to create a fun and easy-to-play game. Specifically, it uses concepts and techniques such as arrays and string-based functions that manipulate and analyze strings to build a game. The object of the Word Find game is to challenge a user to find a single word among seemingly meaningless text (see Figure 8.14). All the code you need to build the Word Find game is shown next:

Trap

If Word Find gives you an error stating that the clear command is not found, go back to the Cygwin setup and install the ncurses package, which is under the Utils category. The ncurses package contains clear.exe and other terminal display utilities.

```c
#include <stdio.h>
#include <string.h>
#include <time.h>
#include <stdlib.h>
#include <ctype.h>

//function prototypes
void checkAnswer(char *, char []);
```

```c
int main()
{
char *strGame[5] = {"ADELANGUAGEFERVZOPIBMOU",
               "ZBPOINTERSKLMLOOPMNOCOT",
               "PODSTRINGGDIWHIEEICERLS",
               "YVCPROGRAMMERWQKNULTHMD",
               "UKUNIXFIMWXIZEQZINPUTEX"};
    char answer[80] = {0};
    int displayed = 0;
    int x;
    int startTime = 0;
    system("clear");

    printf("\n\n\tWord Find\n\n");
    startTime = time(NULL);

    for ( x = 0; x < 5; x++ ) {
        /* DISPLAY TEXT FOR A FEW SECONDS */
        while ( startTime + 3 > time(NULL) ) {
            if ( displayed == 0 ) {
                printf("\nFind a word in: \n\n");
                printf("%s\n\n", strGame[x]);
                displayed = 1;
            } //end if
        } //end while loop

    system("clear");
    printf("\nEnter word found: ");

    gets(answer);
    checkAnswer(strGame[x], answer);

    displayed = 0;
    startTime = time(NULL);
} //end for loop
    return 0;
} //end main

void checkAnswer(char *string1, char string2[])
{
```

```
int x;
/* Convert answer to UPPER CASE to perform a valid comparison*/
for ( x = 0; x <= strlen(string2); x++ )
    string2[x] = toupper(string2[x]);
if ( strstr( string1, string2 ) != 0 && string2[0] != 0 )
    printf("\nGreat job!\n");
else
    printf("\nSorry, word not found!\n");
} //end checkAnswer
```

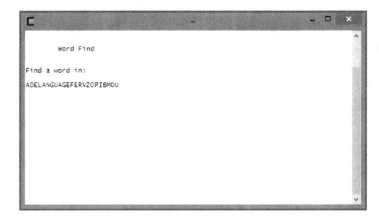

Figure 8.14
Using chapter-based concepts
to build the Word Find program.

Summary

- Strings are groupings of letters, numbers, and many other characters.
- C programmers can create and initialize a string using a character array and a terminating NULL character.
- Assigning a string literal to a character array creates the necessary number of memory elements including the NULL character.
- String literals are a series of characters surrounded by double quotes.
- You can use the printf() function with the %s conversion specifier to print a string to standard output.
- An array of strings is really an array of character pointers.
- The atof() function converts a string to a floating-point number.
- The atoi() function converts a string to an integer.
- Attempting numeric arithmetic on strings can produce unexpected results.

- The strlen() function takes a reference to a string and returns the numeric string length up to the NULL or terminating character, but not including the NULL character.
- The functions tolower() and toupper() are used to convert a single character to lowercase and uppercase, respectively.
- The strcpy() function copies the contents of one string into another.
- The strcat() function concatenates or glues one string to another.
- The strcmp() function is used to compare two strings for equality.

Challenges

1. Create a program that performs the following functions:
   - Uses character arrays to read a user's name from standard input
   - Tells the user how many characters are in her name
   - Displays the user's name in uppercase

2. Create a program that uses the strstr() function to search the string, "When the going gets tough, the tough stay put!" for the following occurrences (display each occurrence found to standard output):
   - "Going"
   - "tou"
   - "ay put!"

3. Build a program that uses an array of strings to store the following names:
   - "Florida"
   - "Oregon"
   - "California"
   - "Georgia"

   Using the preceding array of strings, write your own sort() function to display each state's name in alphabetical order using the strcmp() function.

4. Modify the Word Find game to include one or more of the following suggestions:
   - Add a menu to the Word Find game that allows the user to select a level of difficulty, such as beginning, intermediate, and advanced. The number of seconds the user has to guess or the length of the text in which the user will look for words could determine the level of difficulty.
   - Incorporate multiple words into the text areas.
   - Track the player's score. For example, add 1 point for each word guessed correctly, and subtract 1 point for each word guessed incorrectly.
   - Use the strlen() function to ensure the user's input string is the same length as the hidden word.

Introduction to Data Structures

This chapter introduces a few new computer science concepts for building and using advanced data types (also known as *data structures*), such as structures and unions. It also shows how these user-defined structures assist programmers in defining a more robust, object-aware type. You learn the differences and similarities between structures and unions and how they relate to real-world computing concepts. In addition, you learn more about existing data types and how to convert them from one type to another using typecasting. Specifically, this chapter covers the following topics:

- Structures
- Structures and functions
- Unions
- Typecasting
- Chapter program: Card Shuffle

Structures

Structures are an important computer science concept because they are used throughout the programming and IT world in applications such as relational databases and file processing and in object-oriented programming concepts. Structures, which are considered a data type much like an integer or character, are often referred to as *data structures*. Structures are found in many high-level languages, including Java, C++, Python, and, of course, C. When you combine structures with other data types such as pointers, you can use their by-product to build advanced data structures such as linked lists, stacks, queues, and trees.

Structures are a collection of variables related in nature, but not necessarily in data type. Structures are most commonly used to define an object—a person, a place, a thing—or a record in a database or file. As you will see next, structures use a few new keywords to build a well-defined collection of variables.

The struct Keyword

The first process in creating a structure is to build the structure definition using the struct keyword followed by braces, with individual variables defined as members. Creating a structure is demonstrated with the following program code:

```
struct math {
    int x;
    int y;
    int result;
};
```

The preceding program statements create a structure definition called math that contains three integer-type members. The keyword math is also known as the structure tag, which creates instances of the structure.

Hint

Members of structures are the individual elements or variables that make up a collection of variables. *Structure* tags identify the structure and can be used to create instances of it.

When you create structure definitions using the struct keyword, memory is not allocated for the structure until an instance of the structure is created, as demonstrated next:

```
struct math aProblem;
```

The preceding statement uses the struct keyword and the structure tag (math) to create an instance called aProblem. Creating an instance of a structure is really just creating a variable—in this case, a variable of structure type.

You can initialize a structure instance the same way you would initialize an array. As demonstrated next, I supply an initialization list surrounded by braces, with each item separated by commas:

```
struct math aProblem = { 0, 0, 0};
```

Only after an instance of the structure has been created can members of the structure be accessed via the dot operator (.), also known as dot notation, as demonstrated next:

```
//assign values to members
aProblem.x = 10;
aProblem.y = 10;
aProblem.result = 20;
//print the contents of aProblem
printf("\n%d plus %d", aProblem.x, aProblem.y);
printf(" equals %d\n", aProblem.result);
```

Notice that members of structures are not required to have the same data type, as shown in the following program:

```
#include <stdio.h>
#include <string.h>

struct employee {
    char fname[10];
    char lname[10];
    int id;
    float salary;
};

int main()
{
    //create instance of employee structure
    struct employee emp1;

    //assign values to members
    strcpy(emp1.fname, "Keith");
    strcpy(emp1.lname, "Davenport");
    emp1.id = 123;
    emp1.salary = 50000.00;
```

```
    //print member contents
    printf("\nFirst Name: %s\n", emp1.fname);
    printf("Last Name: %s\n", emp1.lname);
    printf("Employee ID: %d\n", emp1.id);
    printf("Salary: $%.2f\n", emp1.salary);
    return 0;
} //end main
```

Figure 9.1 displays the output of the preceding program.

Figure 9.1
Structures with members of different data types.

The typedef Keyword

The typedef keyword is used to create structure definitions to build an alias relationship with the structure tag (structure name). It provides a shortcut for programmers when creating instances of the structure. To demonstrate the concept of typedef, I reused the program from the preceding section and modified it to include the typedef alias, as shown next:

```
#include <stdio.h>
#include <string.h>

typedef struct employee { //modification here
    char fname[10];
    char lname[10]; int id;
    float salary;
} emp; //modification here
```

```
int main()
{
    //create instance of employee structure using emp
    emp emp1; //modification here

    //assign values to members
    strcpy(emp1.fname, "Keith");
    strcpy(emp1.lname, "Davenport");
    emp1.id = 123;
    emp1.salary = 50000.00;

    //print member contents
    printf("\nFirst Name: %s\n", emp1.fname);
    printf("Last Name: %s\n", emp1.lname);
    printf("Employee ID: %d\n", emp1.id);
    printf("Salary: $%.2f\n", emp1.salary);
    return 0;
} //end main
```

To create a structure alias using typedef, I needed to make minimal changes to my program—specifically, the structure definition, as revealed next:

```
typedef struct employee {
    char fname[10];
    char lname[10];
    int id;
    float salary;
} emp;
```

I included the typedef keyword in the first line of my structure definition. The next modification is at the end of the structure definition, where I tell C that I will use the name emp as my alias for the employee structure. Therefore, I no longer have to use the struct keyword when creating instances of the employee structure. Instead, I can now create instances of my employee structure using the emp name just as I would when declaring a variable using standard data types such as int, char, or double. In other words, I now have a data type called emp! The next set of program statements demonstrates this concept:

```
emp emp1; //I can now do this
struct employee emp1; //Instead of doing this
```

To create instances of the employee structure using aliases, supply the alias name followed by a new variable name.

Arrays of Structures

The process of creating and working with an array of structures is similar to working with arrays containing other data types, such as integers, characters, or floats.

APPLIED STRUCTURES

If you are familiar with database concepts, you can think of a single structure as one database record. To demonstrate, consider an employee structure that contains members (attributes) of an employee, such as name, employee ID, hire date, salary, and so on. Moreover, if a single instance of an employee structure represents one employee database record, an array of employee structures is, for example, equivalent to a database table containing multiple employee records.

To create an array of structures, supply the desired number of array elements surrounded by brackets after the structure definition, as shown next:

```
typedef struct employee {
    char fname[10];
    char lname[10];
    int id;
    float salary;
} emp;
emp emp1[5];
```

To access individual elements in a structure array, you need to provide the array element number surrounded by brackets. To access individual structure members, you need to supply the dot operator followed by the structure member name, as revealed in the next segment of code, which uses the strcpy() function to copy the text "Spencer" into the memory reserved by the structure member:

```
strcpy(emp1[0].fname, "Spencer");
```

The next program and its output, shown in Figure 9.2, demonstrate arrays of structures in more detail:

```
#include <stdio.h>
#include <string.h>

typedef struct scores {
    char name[10];
    int score;
} s;
```

```c
int main()
{
    s highScores[3];
    int x;

    //assign values to members
    strcpy(highScores[0].name, "Hunter");
    highScores[0].score = 40768;
    strcpy(highScores[1].name, "Kenya");
    highScores[1].score = 38565;
    strcpy(highScores[2].name, "Apollo");
    highScores[2].score = 35985;

    //print array content
    printf("\nTop 3 High Scores\n");
    for ( x = 0; x < 3; x++ )
        printf("\n%s\t%d\n", highScores[x].name, highScores[x].score);
    return 0;
} //end main
```

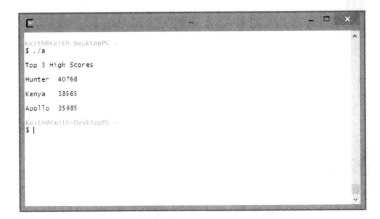

Figure 9.2
Creating and using arrays of structures.

Structures and Functions

To utilize the power of structures, you need to understand how to pass them to functions for processing. You can pass structures to functions in a multitude of ways, including passing by value for read-only access and passing by reference for modifying structure member contents.

> **Hint**
>
> *Passing by value* protects an incoming variable's value by sending a copy of the original data rather than the actual variable to the function. *Passing by reference* sends a variable's memory address to a function, which allows statements in the function to modify the original variable's memory contents.

Passing Structures by Value

Like any parameter passed by value, C makes a copy of the incoming structure variable for the function to use. Any modifications made to the parameter within the receiving function are not made to the original variable's value. To pass a structure by value to a function, you need only to supply the function prototype and function definition with the structure tag (or the alias if typedef is used). This process is demonstrated in the next program and its corresponding output in Figure 9.3:

```c
#include <stdio.h>
#include <string.h>

typedef struct employee {
    int id;
    char name[10];
    float salary;
} e;

void processEmp(e); //supply prototype with structure alias name

int main()
{
    e emp1 = {0,0,0}; //initialize members
    processEmp(emp1); //pass structure by value

    printf("\nID: %d\n", emp1.id);
    printf("Name: %s\n", emp1.name);
    printf("Salary: $%.2f\n", emp1.salary);
    return 0;
} //end main

void processEmp(e emp) //receives a copy of the structure
{
```

```
    emp.id = 123;
    strcpy(emp.name, "Sheila");
    emp.salary = 65000.00;
} //end processEmp
```

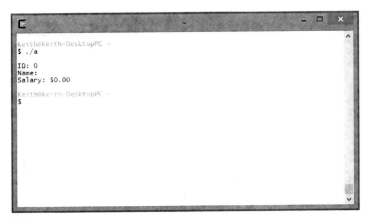

Figure 9.3
Passing a structure by value to a function does not change the original values of the structure's members.

As you can see in Figure 9.3, the structure's members still contain their initialization values even though the structure members appear to be updated in the processEmp() function. The structure's original member contents weren't really modified. In fact, only a copy of the structure's members were accessed and modified. In other words, passing by value causes the processEmp() function to modify a copy of the structure rather than its original member contents.

Passing Structures by Reference

Passing structures by reference requires a bit more knowledge and adherence to C rules and regulations. Before learning how to pass structures by reference, you need to learn a second means for accessing members of structures. In this approach, you can access members via the structure pointer operator (->). The structure pointer operator is a dash followed by the greater-than sign with no spaces in between, as demonstrated next:

```
emp->salary = 80000.00;
```

The structure pointer operator is used to access a structure member through a pointer. This form of member access is useful when you have created a pointer of structure type and need to indirectly reference a member's value.

The next program demonstrates how a pointer of structure type is created and its members are accessed via the structure pointer operator:

```c
#include <stdio.h>
#include <string.h>

int main()
{
    typedef struct player {
    char name[15];
    float score;
    } p;

    p aPlayer = {0, 0}; //create instance of structure
    p *ptrPlayer; //create a pointer of structure type
    ptrPlayer = &aPlayer; //assign address to pointer of structure type

    strcpy(ptrPlayer->name, "Pinball Wizard"); //access through indirection
    ptrPlayer->score = 1000000.00;

    printf("\nPlayer: %s\n", ptrPlayer->name);
    printf("Score: %.0f\n", ptrPlayer->score);
    return 0;
} //end main
```

When you understand the structure pointer operator, passing structures by reference is really quite easy. For the most part, structures passed by reference follow the same rules as any other variable passed by reference. Simply tell the function prototype and its definition to expect a pointer of structure type and remember to use the structure pointer operator (->) inside your functions to access each structure member.

To further demonstrate these concepts, study the next program's implementation:

```c
#include <stdio.h>
#include <string.h>

typedef struct employee {
    int id;
    char name[10];
    float salary;
} emp;
```

```
void processEmp(emp *);

int main()
{
    emp emp1 = {0, 0, 0};
    emp *ptrEmp;
    ptrEmp = &emp1;
    processEmp(ptrEmp);

    printf("\nID: %d\n", ptrEmp->id);
    printf("Name: %s\n", ptrEmp->name);
    printf("Salary: $%.2f\n", ptrEmp->salary);
    return 0;
} //end main

void processEmp(emp *e)
{
    e->id = 123;
    strcpy(e->name, "Sheila");
    e->salary = 65000.00;
} //end processEmp
```

Figure 9.4 demonstrates the output of the previous program and more specifically demonstrates how passing by reference allows functions to modify the original contents of variables, including structure variables.

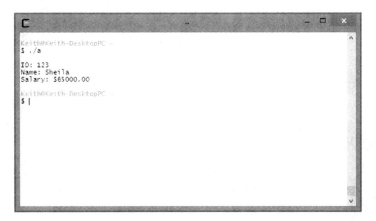

Figure 9.4
Passing structures by reference allows a called function to modify the original contents of the structure's members.

Passing Arrays of Structures

Unless otherwise specified, passing arrays of structures to functions is automatically passing by reference; it is also known as passing by address. This is true because an array name is really nothing more than a pointer!

To pass an array of structures, simply supply the function prototype with a pointer to the structure, as demonstrated in the next modified program:

```c
#include <stdio.h>
#include <string.h>

typedef struct employee {
    int id;
    char name[10];
    float salary;
} e;

void processEmp( e * ); //supply prototype with pointer of structure type

int main()
{
    e emp1[3] = {0,0,0};
    int x;
    processEmp( emp1 ); //pass array name, which is a pointer
    for ( x = 0; x < 3; x++ ) {
        printf("\nID: %d\n", emp1[x].id); printf("Name: %s\n", emp1[x].name);
        printf("Salary: $%.2f\n\n", emp1[x].salary);
    } //end loop
    return 0;
} //end main

void processEmp( e * emp ) //function receives a pointer
{
    emp[0].id = 123;
    strcpy(emp[0].name, "Sheila");
    emp[0].salary = 65000.00;
    emp[1].id = 234;
    strcpy(emp[1].name, "Hunter");
    emp[1].salary = 28000.00;
    emp[2].id = 456;
```

```
    strcpy(emp[2].name, "Kenya");
    emp[2].salary = 48000.00;
} //end processEmp
```

As shown in Figure 9.5, the processEmp() function can modify the structure's original member contents using pass by reference techniques.

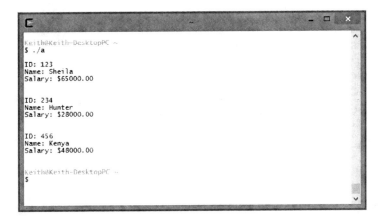

Figure 9.5
Passing an array of structures by reference.

Trick

You do not need to use pointers when passing an array of structures to a function because array names *are* pointers! You can also pass structure arrays by reference simply by telling the function prototype and function definition to receive an array of structure type using empty brackets, as demonstrated next:

```
void processEmp( e [] ); //function prototype
void processEmp( e emp[] ) //function definition
{
}
```

Passing an array to a function is actually passing the first memory address of the array. This type of action produces a simulated pass by reference outcome that allows the user to modify each structure and its members directly.

Unions

Although similar to structures in design and use, *unions* provide a more economical way to build objects with attributes (members) that are not required to be in use at the same time. Whereas structures reserve separate memory segments for each member when they are created, a union reserves a single memory space for its largest member, thereby providing a memory-saving feature for members to share the same memory space.

Unions are created with the keyword union and contain member definitions similar to that of structures. The next block of program code creates a union definition for a phone book:

```c
union phoneBook {
    char *name;
    char *number;
    char *address;
};
```

Like structures, union members are accessed via the dot operator, as the next program demonstrates:

```c
#include <stdio.h>

union phoneBook
{
    char *name;
    char *number;
    char *address;
};

struct magazine {
    char *name;
    char *author;
    int isbn;
};

int main()
{
    union phoneBook aBook;
    struct magazine aMagazine;
    printf("\nUnion Details\n");
    printf("Address for aBook.name: %p\n", &aBook.name);
    printf("Address for aBook.number: %p\n", &aBook.number);
    printf("Address for aBook.address: %p\n", &aBook.address);
```

```
    printf("\nStructure Details\n");
    printf("Address for aMagazine.name: %p\n", &aMagazine.name);
    printf("Address for aMagazine.author: %p\n", &aMagazine.author);
    printf("Address for aMagazine.isbn: %p\n", &aMagazine.isbn);
    return 0;
} //end main
```

The output of the preceding program is shown in Figure 9.6, which reveals how memory allocation is conducted between unions and structures. Each member of the union shares the same memory space.

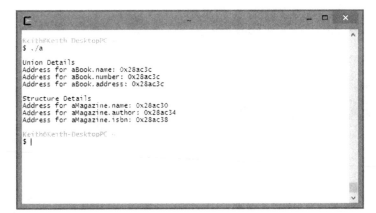

Figure 9.6
Comparing memory allocation between structures and unions.

Typecasting

Although it is not supported by all high-level programming languages, typecasting is a powerful feature of C. *Typecasting* enables C programmers to force one variable of a certain type to be another type, an important consideration especially when dealing with integer division. For all its power, typecasting is simple to use. As demonstrated next, just surround a datatype name with parentheses followed by the data or variable for which you want to typecast:

```
int x = 12;
int y = 5;
float result = 0;
result = (float) x / (float) y;
```

Hint

Hollywood does a lot of typecasting!

The next program and its output (shown in Figure 9.7) further demonstrate the use of typecasting. In addition, they show what happens when typecasting is not leveraged during integer division:

```c
#include <stdio.h>

int main()
{
    int x = 12;
    int y = 5;
    printf("\nWithout Typecasting\n");
    printf("12 \\ 5 = %.2f\n", x/y);
    printf("\nWith Typecasting\n");
    printf("12 \\ 5 = %.2f\n", (float) x / (float) y);
    return 0;
} //end main
```

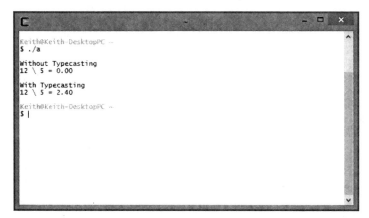

Figure 9.7
Conducting integer division with and without typecasting.

Trick

Remember that the backslash (\) is a reserved and special character in the `printf()` function. To incorporate a backslash character in your output, use the \\ conversion specifier shown next:

```c
printf("12 \\ 5 = %.2f\n", (float) x / (float) y);
```

As you might expect, typecasting is not limited to numbers. You can also typecast numbers to characters and characters to numbers, as shown next:

```c
#include <stdio.h>

int main()
{
    int number = 86;
    char letter = 'M';

    printf("\n86 typecasted to char is: %c\n", (char) number);
    printf("\n'M' typecasted to int is: %d\n ", (int) letter);
    return 0;
} //end main
```

Figure 9.8 demonstrates the output from the preceding program in which a number is typecasted to a character and a character is typecasted to a number.

Hint

C always prints the ASCII equivalent of a letter when using the %n conversion specifier with a character equivalent. In addition, C always prints the character equivalent of an ASCII number when using the %c conversion specifier with an ASCII equivalent.

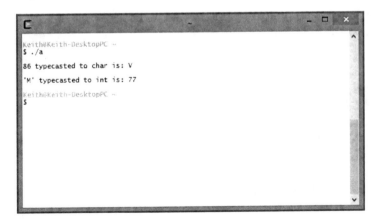

Figure 9.8
Typecasting numbers to characters and characters to numbers.

Chapter Program: Card Shuffle

The Card Shuffle program, as shown in Figure 9.9, uses many chapter-based concepts, such as structures, arrays of structures, and passing structures to functions, to build an easy card-shuffling program. Specifically, the Card Shuffle program initializes 52 poker cards using an array of structures. It then uses various techniques, such as random numbers and user-defined functions, to build a shuffle routine, which deals five random cards after shuffling.

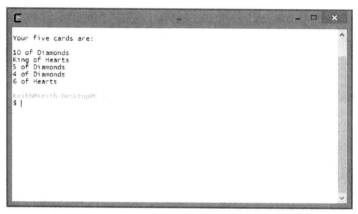

Figure 9.9
Using chapter-based concepts to build the Card Shuffle program.

After studying the Card Shuffle program, you should be able to use it in your own card games to shuffle and deal cards for Poker games and others, such as Five Card Draw and Blackjack.

Trap

If you get an error message in Card Shuffle stating that the clear command is not found, go back to the Cygwin setup and install the ncurses package, which is under the Utils category. The ncurses package contains clear.exe and other terminal display utilities.

All the code required to build the Card Shuffle program is shown next:

```
#include <stdio.h>
#include <stdlib.h>
#include <time.h>
#include <string.h>
```

```
//define new data type
typedef struct deck {
    char type[10];
    char used;
    int value;
} aDeck; //end type

//function prototype
void shuffle( aDeck * );

int main()
{
    int x,y;
    aDeck myDeck[52];
    srand( time( NULL ) );

    //initialize structure array
    for ( x = 0; x < 3; x++ ) {
        for ( y = 0; y < 13; y++ ) {
            switch (x) {
                case 0:
                    strcpy(myDeck[y].type, "Diamonds");
                    myDeck[y].value = y;
                    myDeck[y].used = 'n';
                    break;
                case 1:
                    strcpy(myDeck[y + 13].type, "Clubs");
                    myDeck[y + 13].value = y;
                    myDeck[y + 13].used = 'n';
                    break;
                case 2:
                    strcpy(myDeck[y + 26].type, "Hearts");
                    myDeck[y + 26].value = y;
                    myDeck[y + 26].used = 'n';
                    break;
                case 3:
                    strcpy(myDeck[y + 39].type, "Spades");
                    myDeck[y + 39].value = y;
                    myDeck[y + 39].used = 'n';
                    break;
```

```
            } //end switch
        } //end inner loop
    } //end outer loop

    shuffle( myDeck );
    return 0;
} //end main

void shuffle( aDeck * thisDeck )
{
    int x;
    int iRnd;
    int found = 0;
    system("clear");

    printf("\nYour five cards are: \n\n");
    while ( found < 5 ) {
        iRnd = rand() % 51;
        if ( thisDeck[iRnd].used == 'n' ) {
            switch (thisDeck[iRnd].value) {
                case 12:
                    printf("Ace of %s\n", thisDeck[iRnd].type);
                    break;
                case 11:
                    printf("King of %s\n", thisDeck[iRnd].type);
                    break;
                case 10:
                    printf("Queen of %s\n", thisDeck[iRnd].type);
                    break;
                case 9:
                    printf("Jack of %s\n", thisDeck[iRnd].type);
                    break;
                default:
                    printf("%d of ", thisDeck[iRnd].value + 2);
                    printf("%s\n", thisDeck[iRnd].type);
                    break;
            } //end switch
            thisDeck[iRnd].used = 'y';
            found = found + 1;
```

```
      } //end if
    } //end while loop
} //end shuffle
```

Summary

- Structures are a collection of variables related in nature, but not necessarily in data type.
- Structures are most commonly used to define an object—a person, a place, a thing—or a similar record in a database or file.
- The first process in creating a structure is to build the structure definition using the `struct` keyword followed by braces, with individual variables defined as members.
- Members of structures are the individual elements or variables that make up a collection of variables.
- Structure tags identify the structure and can create instances of the structure.
- When you create structure definitions using the `struct` keyword, memory is not allocated for the structure until you create an instance of the structure.
- The `typedef` keyword is used to create structure definitions to build an alias relationship with the structure tag (structure name). It provides a shortcut for programmers when creating instances of the structure.
- To create an array of structures, supply the desired number of array elements surrounded by brackets after the structure definition.
- You can pass structures to functions via pass by value for read-only access and pass by reference for modifying structure member contents.
- Passing by value protects an incoming variable's value by sending a copy of the original data rather than the actual variable to the function.
- Passing by reference sends a variable's memory address to a function, which allows statements in the function to modify the original variable's memory contents.
- The structure pointer operator is a dash followed by the greater-than sign with no space in between (`->`).
- You use the structure pointer operator to access a structure member through a pointer.
- Passing arrays of structures to functions is automatically passing by reference; it is also known as passing by address. This is true because an array name is a pointer.
- Unions provide a more economical way to build objects with attributes by reserving a single memory space for its largest member.
- Typecasting enables C programmers to force one variable of a certain type to be another type.

1. Create a structure called car with the following members:
   - make
   - model
   - year
   - miles

2. Create an instance of the car structure named myCar, and assign data to each of the members. Print the contents of each member to standard output using the printf() function.

3. Using the car structure from Challenge 1, create a structure array with three elements named myCars. Populate each structure in the array with your favorite car model information. Use a for loop to print each structure detail in the array.

4. Create a program that uses a structure array to hold contact information for your friends. The program should allow the user to enter up to five friends and print the phone book's current entries. Create functions to add entries in the phone book and to print valid phone book entries. Do not display phone book entries that are invalid or NULL (0).

10

Dynamic Memory Allocation

In this chapter, I show you how C uses system resources to allocate, reallocate, and free memory. You learn basic memory concepts and how C library functions and operators can take advantage of system resources, such as RAM and virtual memory.

Specifically, this chapter covers the following topics:

- Dynamic memory concepts
- The `sizeof` operator
- The `malloc()` function
- The `calloc()` and `realloc()` functions
- Chapter program: Math Quiz

Dynamic Memory Concepts

This chapter is dedicated to discussing dynamic memory concepts, such as allocating, reallocating, and freeing memory using the functions `malloc()`, `calloc()`, `realloc()`, and `free()`. This section specifically reviews essential memory concepts that directly relate to how these functions receive and use memory.

Software programs, including operating systems, use a variety of memory implementations, including virtual memory and RAM. Random Access Memory (RAM) provides a volatile solution for allocating, storing, and retrieving data. RAM is considered volatile because of its inability to store data after the computer loses power (shuts down). Another volatile memory storage area is called virtual memory. Basically, virtual memory is a reserved section of your hard disk where the operating system can swap memory segments. Accessing virtual memory is slow compared to accessing physical RAM, but it provides a place to move data when physical memory runs low. Increasing memory resources through virtual memory gives the operating system a method, albeit an inefficient one, to meet dynamic memory demands.

> **Hint**
>
> *Virtual memory* frees physical RAM by swapping data to and from the hard disk.

Stack and Heap

Using a combination of RAM and virtual memory, all software programs use their own area of memory called the *stack*. Every time a function is called in a program, the function's variables and parameters are pushed onto the program's memory stack and then pushed off or "popped" when the function has completed or returned.

> **Hint**
>
> Used for storing variable and parameter contents, *memory stacks* are dynamic groupings of memory that grow and shrink as each program allocates and de-allocates memory.

After software programs have terminated, memory is returned for reuse for other software and system programs. Moreover, the operating system is responsible for managing this realm of unallocated memory, known as the *heap*. Software programs that can leverage memory-allocating functions such as `malloc()`, `calloc()`, and `realloc()` use the heap.

Once a program frees memory, it is returned to the heap for further use by the same program or other programs.

In a nutshell, memory-allocating functions and the heap are extremely important to C programmers because they enable you to control a program's memory consumption and allocation. The remainder of this chapter shows you how to retrieve and return memory to and from the heap.

The sizeof Operator

There are times when you need to know, in terms of memory usage, the size of a variable or data type. This is especially important in C, because C enables programmers to create memory resources dynamically. More specifically, it is imperative for C programmers to know how many bytes a system uses to store data, such as integers, floats, or doubles, because not all systems use the same amount of space for storing data. The C standard library provides the sizeof operator to assist programmers in this type of situation. When used in your programs, the sizeof operator helps you build a more system-independent software program.

The sizeof operator takes a variable name or data type as an argument and returns the number of bytes required to store the data in memory. The next program, and its output shown in Figure 10.1, demonstrates a simple use of the sizeof operator:

```
#include <stdio.h>

int main()
{
    int x;
    float f;
    double d;
    char c;
    typedef struct employee {
        int id;
        char *name;
        float salary;
    } e;
```

```
    printf("\nSize of integer: %d bytes\n", sizeof(x));
    printf("Size of float: %d bytes\n", sizeof(f));
    printf("Size of double %d bytes\n", sizeof(d));
    printf("Size of char %d byte\n", sizeof(c));
    printf("Size of employee structure: %d bytes\n", sizeof(e));
    return 0;
} //end main
```

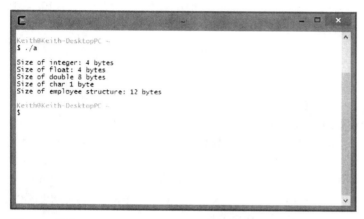

Figure 10.1
Using the sizeof operator to determine storage requirements.

The sizeof operator can take either a variable name or a data type, as shown next:

```
int x;
    printf("\nSize of integer: %d bytes\n", sizeof(x)); //valid variable name
    printf("\nSize of integer: %d bytes\n", sizeof(int)); //valid data type
```

The sizeof operator can also be used to determine the memory requirements of arrays. Using simple arithmetic, you can determine how many elements are contained in an array by dividing the array size by the size of the array data type, as demonstrated in the next program, whose output is shown in Figure 10.2:

```
#include <stdio.h>

int main()
{
    int array[10];
```

```
    printf("\nSize of array: %d bytes\n", sizeof(array));
    printf("Number of elements in array ");
    printf("%d\n", sizeof(array) / sizeof(int));
    return 0;
} //end main
```

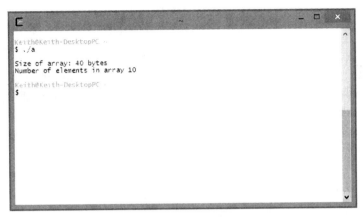

Figure 10.2
Using the sizeof operator and simple arithmetic to determine the number of elements in an array.

The malloc() Function

Sometimes it is impossible to know exactly how much memory your program needs for a given function. Fixed-sized arrays may not be large enough to hold the amount of data you are attempting to store. For example, what would happen if you created an eight-element, fixed-size character array to hold a user's name, and the user enters the name Alexandria— a 10-character name (with an 11th character required for NULL)? Best-case scenario: you incorporated error checking into your program to prevent a user from entering a string larger than eight characters. Worst-case scenario: the user's information is sent elsewhere in memory, potentially overwriting other data.

There are many reasons for dynamically creating and using memory, such as creating and reading strings from standard input, dynamic arrays, and other dynamic data structures such as linked lists. C provides a few functions for creating dynamic memory, one of which is the malloc() function. The malloc() function is part of the standard library <stdlib.h> and takes a number as an argument. When executed, malloc() attempts to retrieve designated memory segments from the heap and returns a pointer that is the starting point for the memory reserved. Basic malloc() use is demonstrated in the next program:

```
#include <stdio.h>
#include <stdlib.h>

int main()
{
    char *name;
    name = malloc(80);
    return 0;
} //end main
```

The preceding program's use of malloc() is not quite complete because some C compilers may require that you perform typecasting when assigning dynamic memory to a variable. To eliminate potential compiler warnings, I will modify the previous program to simply use a pointer of type char in a typecast, as demonstrated next:

```
#include <stdio.h>
#include <stdlib.h>

int main()
{
    char *name;
    name = (char *) malloc(80);
    return 0;
} //end main
```

Hint

The malloc() function returns a NULL pointer if it is unsuccessful in allocating memory.

Better yet, you should be more specific when creating dynamic memory by explicitly telling the system the size of the data type for which we are requesting memory. In other words, you should incorporate the sizeof operator in your dynamic memory allocation, as shown next:

```
#include <stdio.h>
#include <stdlib.h>

int main()
{
```

```
    char *name;
    name = (char *) malloc(80 * sizeof(char));
    return 0;
} //end main
```

Using the `sizeof` operator explicitly tells the system that you want 80 bytes of type `char`, which happens to be a one-byte data type on most systems.

You should also always check that `malloc()` was successful before attempting to use the memory. To test the `malloc()` function's outcome, simply use an `if` condition to test for a NULL pointer, as revealed next:

```
#include <stdio.h>
#include <stdlib.h>

int main()
{
    char *name;
    name = (char *) malloc(80 * sizeof(char));

    if ( name == NULL ) {
        printf("\nOut of memory!\n");
        return 1; }
    else {
        printf("\nMemory allocated.\n");
        return 0; }
} //end main
```

After studying the preceding program, you can see that the keyword NULL is used to compare the pointer. If the pointer is NULL, the `malloc()` function was not successful in allocating memory, and the program returns a 1 (indicating an error condition) to the operating system. If the `malloc()` operation is successful, the memory is allocated and the program returns a 0 (indicating normal termination) to the operating system.

Trap

Always check for valid results when attempting to allocate memory. Failure to test the pointer returned by memory-allocating functions such as `malloc()` can result in abnormal software or system behavior.

Managing Strings with malloc()

As mentioned in Chapter 8, "Strings," dynamic memory allocation enables programmers to create and use strings when reading information from standard input. To do so, simply use the malloc() function and assign its result to a pointer of char type prior to reading information from the keyboard.

Using malloc() to create and read strings from standard input is demonstrated in the next program (see Figure 10.3).

```c
#include <stdio.h>
#include <stdlib.h>

int main()
{
    char *name;
    name = (char *) malloc(80*sizeof(char));

    if ( name != NULL ) {
        printf("\nEnter your name: ");
        gets(name);
        printf("\nHi %s\n", name);
    } //end if
    return 0;
} //end main
```

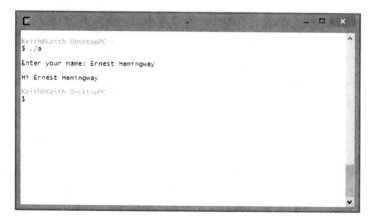

Figure 10.3
Using dynamic memory to read character strings from standard input.

This program allows a user to enter up to an 80-character name, the amount of storage requested by the `malloc()` function, for the character string.

Freeing Memory

Good programming practice dictates that you free memory after using it. For this reason, the C standard library offers the `free()` function, which takes a pointer as an argument and frees the memory that the pointer refers to. This lets your operating system reuse the memory for other software applications or other `malloc()` function calls, as demonstrated next:

```
#include <stdio.h>
#include <stdlib.h>

int main()
{
    char *name;
    name = (char *) malloc(80*sizeof(char));

    if ( name != NULL ) {
        printf("\nEnter your name: ");
        gets(name);
        printf("\nHi %s\n", name);
        free(name); //free memory resources
    } //end if
    return 0;
} //end main
```

Freeing memory allocated by functions such as `malloc()` is an important housekeeping duty of C programmers. Even with today's memory-rich systems, it's a good idea to free memory as soon as you no longer need it because the more memory you consume, the less that is available for other processes. If you forget to release allocated or used memory in your programs, most operating systems clean up for you. This cleanup only applies after your program terminates, however. It is the programmer's responsibility, therefore, to free memory once it is no longer needed. Failure to release memory in your programs can result in unnecessary or wasted memory that is not returned to the heap, also known as a *memory leak*. If your program keeps allocating more memory and does not free it, the leak could result in application failure and system performance degradation.

Working with Memory Segments

Individual memory segments acquired by `malloc()` can be treated much like array members.
These memory segments can be referenced with indexes; see the next program, whose output is
shown in Figure 10.4:

```c
#include <stdio.h>
#include <stdlib.h>

int main()
{
    int *numbers;
    int x;
    numbers = (int *) malloc(5 * sizeof(int));

    if ( numbers == NULL )
        return 1; //return nonzero value if malloc is not successful

    numbers[0] = 100;
    numbers[1] = 200;
    numbers[2] = 300;
    numbers[3] = 400;
    numbers[4] = 500;

    printf("\nIndividual memory segments initialized to:\n");
    for ( x = 0; x < 5; x++ )
        printf("numbers[%d] = %d\n", x, numbers[x]);
    return 0;
} //end main
```

To initialize and access segments of memory, simply supply the pointer name with an index. To
reiterate, you can access memory segments through indexes, similar to array elements. This is a
useful and powerful concept for dissecting chunks of memory.

Figure 10.4
Using indexes and array concepts to work with memory segments.

The calloc() and realloc() Functions

Another memory-allocating tool is the C standard library <stdlib.h> function calloc(). Like the malloc() function, the calloc() function attempts to grab contiguous segments of memory from the heap. The calloc() function takes two arguments: the first determines the number of memory segments needed, and the second is the size of the data type.

A basic implementation of the calloc() function is established in the next program:

```
#include <stdio.h>
#include <stdlib.h>

int main()
{
    int *numbers;
    numbers = (int *) calloc(10, sizeof(int));

    if ( numbers == NULL )
        return 1; //return 1 if calloc is not successful
    return 0; //return 0 if calloc is successful
} //end main
```

I can use the calloc() function to obtain a chunk of memory to hold 10 integer data types by passing two arguments. The first argument tells calloc() I want 10 contiguous memory segments, and the second argument tells C that the data types need to be the size of an integer data type on the machine it's running.

The main benefit of using `calloc()` rather than `malloc()` is `calloc()`'s capability to initialize each memory segment allocated. This is an important feature because `malloc()` requires that the programmer be responsible for initializing memory before using it.

At first glance, both `malloc()` and `calloc()` appear to be dynamic in memory allocation, and they are to some degree, yet they fall somewhat short in their ability to expand memory originally allocated. For example, say you allocated five integer memory segments and filled them with data. Later, the program requires that you add five more memory segments to the original block allocated by `malloc()` while preserving the original contents. This is an interesting dilemma. You could, of course, allocate more memory using a separate pointer, but that would not enable you to treat both memory blocks as a contiguous memory area; therefore, you wouldn't be able to access all memory segments as a single array. Fortunately, the `realloc()` function provides a way to expand contiguous blocks of memory while preserving the original contents.

As shown next, the `realloc()` function takes two arguments for parameters and returns a pointer as output:

```
newPointer = realloc(oldPointer, 10 * sizeof(int));
```

`realloc()`'s first argument takes the original pointer set by `malloc()` or `calloc()`. The second argument describes the total amount of memory you want to allocate.

Like the `malloc()` and `calloc()` functions, `realloc()` is an easy-to-use function, but it does require some spot-checking after it executes. Specifically, there are three scenarios for `realloc()`'s outcome, which Table 10.1.shows.

TABLE 10.1 POSSIBLE REALLOC() OUTCOMES

Scenario	Outcome
Successful without move	Same pointer returned
Successful with move	New pointer returned
Not successful	NULL pointer returned

If `realloc()` is successful in expanding the contiguous memory, it returns the original pointer set by `malloc()` or `calloc()`. There will be times, however, when `realloc()` is unable to expand the original contiguous memory and will, therefore, seek another area in memory where it can allocate the number of contiguous memory segments for both the previous data and the new memory requested. When this happens, `realloc()` copies the original memory contents into the new contiguous memory locations and returns a new pointer to the new starting location. Be aware that sometimes `realloc()` will not be successful in its attempts to expand contiguous memory and ultimately will return a NULL pointer.

Your best bet for testing the outcome of `realloc()` is testing for NULL. If a NULL pointer is not returned, you can assign the pointer back to the old pointer, which then contains the starting address of the expanded contiguous memory.

The concept of expanding contiguous memory and testing `realloc()`'s outcome is demonstrated in the next program, with the output shown in Figure 10.5:

```c
#include<stdio.h>
#include<stdlib.h>

int main()
{
    int *number;
    int *newNumber;
    int x;

    number = malloc(sizeof(int) * 5);

    if ( number == NULL ) {
        printf("\nOut of memory!\n");
        return 1;
    } //end if

    printf("\nOriginal memory:\n");

    for ( x = 0; x < 5; x++ ) {
        number[x] = x * 100;
        printf("number[%d] = %d\n", x, number[x]);
    } //end for loop

    newNumber = realloc(number, 10 * sizeof(int));

    if ( newNumber == NULL ) {
        printf("\nOut of memory!\n");
        return 1;
    }
    else
        number = newNumber;
    //initialize new memory only
```

```
for ( x = 5; x < 10; x++ )
    number[x] = x * 100;

printf("\nExpanded memory:\n");

for ( x = 0; x < 10; x++ )
    printf("number[%d] = %d\n", x, number[x]);

//free memory
free(number);
return 0;
} //end main
```

After studying the preceding program and Figure 10.5, you can see that realloc() is quite useful for expanding contiguous memory while preserving original memory contents.

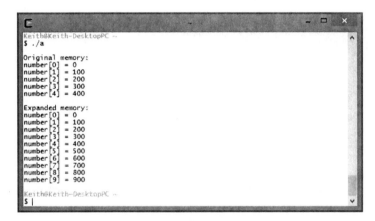

Figure 10.5
Using realloc() to expand contiguous memory segments.

Chapter Program: Math Quiz

Shown in Figure 10.6, the Math Quiz game uses memory allocation techniques, such as the calloc() and free() functions, to build a fun and dynamic quiz that tests the player's ability to answer basic addition problems. After studying the Math Quiz program, you can use your own dynamic memory allocation and random number techniques to build fun quiz programs of any nature.

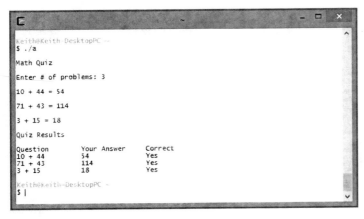

Figure 10.6
Using chapter-based concepts to build the Math Quiz.

All the code required to build the Math Quiz game is demonstrated next:

```
#include <stdio.h>
#include <stdlib.h>
#include <time.h>

int main()
{
    int response;
    int *answer;
    int *op1;
    int *op2;
    char *result;
    int x;
    srand(time(NULL));

    printf("\nMath Quiz\n\n");
    printf("Enter # of problems: ");
    scanf("%d", &response);

    /* Based on the number of questions the user wishes to take,
    allocate enough memory to hold question data. */
    op1 = (int *) calloc(response, sizeof(int));
    op2 = (int *) calloc(response, sizeof(int));
```

```c
    answer = (int *) calloc(response, sizeof(int));
    result = (char *) calloc(response, sizeof(char));

    if ( op1 == NULL || op2 == NULL || answer == NULL || result == NULL ) {
        printf("\nOut of Memory!\n");
        return 1;
    } //end if

    //display random addition problems
    for ( x = 0; x < response; x++ ) {
        op1[x] = rand() % 100;
        op2[x] = rand() % 100;
        printf("\n%d + %d = ", op1[x], op2[x]);
        scanf("%d", &answer[x]);
        if ( answer[x] == op1[x] + op2[x] )
            result[x] = 'c';
        else
            result[x] = 'i';
    } //end for loop

    printf("\nQuiz Results\n");
    printf("\nQuestion\tYour Answer\tCorrect\n");

    //print the results of the quiz
    for ( x = 0; x < response; x++ ) {
        if ( result[x] == 'c' )
            printf("%d + %d\t\t%d\t\tYes\n", op1[x], op2[x], answer[x]);
        else
            printf("%d + %d\t\t%d\t\tNo\n", op1[x], op2[x], answer[x]);
    } //end for loop

    //free memory
    free(op1);
    free(op2);
    free(answer);
    free(result);
    return 0;
} //end main
```

Summary

- Random Access Memory (RAM) provides a volatile solution for allocating, storing, and retrieving data. RAM is considered volatile because of its inability to store data after the computer loses power (shuts down).
- Another volatile memory storage area called virtual memory is a reserved section of the hard disk where the operating system can swap memory segments.
- Virtual memory is not as efficient as RAM, but it does provide additional memory resources to the CPU if needed.
- Memory stacks are dynamic groupings of memory that grow and shrink as each program allocates and deallocates memory. They are used for storing contents of variables and parameters.
- The heap is an area of unused memory that the operating system manages.
- The `sizeof` operator takes a variable name or a data type as an argument and returns the number of bytes required to store the data in memory.
- The `sizeof` operator can also be used to determine the memory requirements of arrays.
- The `malloc()` function attempts to retrieve designated memory segments from the heap and returns a pointer that is the starting point for the memory reserved.
- The `malloc()` function returns a `NULL` pointer if it is unsuccessful in allocating memory.
- Individual memory segments acquired by `malloc()` can be treated much like array members; these memory segments can be referenced with indexes.
- The `free()` function takes a pointer as an argument and frees the memory to which the pointer refers.
- Like the `malloc()` function, the `calloc()` function attempts to grab contiguous segments of memory from the heap. The `calloc()` function takes two arguments: the first determines the number of memory segments needed, and the second is the size of the data type.
- The main benefit of using `calloc()` rather than `malloc()` is `calloc()`'s ability to initialize each memory segment allocated.
- The `realloc()` function provides a feature for expanding contiguous blocks of memory while preserving the original contents.

1. Create a program that uses `malloc()` to allocate a chunk of memory to hold a string no larger than 80 characters. Prompt the user to enter his favorite movie. Read his response with `scanf()`, and assign the data to your newly allocated memory. Display the user's favorite movie back to standard output.

2. Using the `calloc()` function, write a program that reads a user's name from standard input. Use a loop to iterate through the memory allocated, counting the number of characters in the user's name. The loop should stop when a memory segment is reached that was not used for reading and storing the user's name. (Remember, `calloc()` initializes all memory allocated.) Print the number of characters in the user's name to standard output.

3. Create a phone book program that enables users to enter names and phone numbers of friends and acquaintances. Create a structure to hold contact information, and use `calloc()` to reserve the first memory segment. The user should be able to add or modify phone book entries through a menu. Use the `realloc()` function to add contiguous memory segments to the original memory block when a user adds a new phone book entry.

11

File Input and Output

In this chapter, I show you how to open, read, and write information to data files using functions from the standard input/output (`<stdio.h>`) library. You also learn essential data file hierarchy concepts and how C uses file streams to manage data files.

Specifically, this chapter covers the following topics:

- Introduction to data files
- Bits and bytes
- File streams
- `goto` and error handling
- Chapter program: Character Roster

Introduction to Data Files

Assuming you've been reading the chapters of this book in order, you've already learned the basics of utilizing C and volatile memory storage devices for saving, retrieving, and editing data. Specifically, you know that variables are used to manage data in volatile memory areas, such as random access memory and virtual memory, and that memory can be dynamically obtained for temporarily storing data.

Despite the obvious importance of volatile memory such as Random Access Memory (RAM), it does have its drawbacks when it comes to long-term data storage. When data needs to be archived or stored in nonvolatile memory areas such as a hard disk, programmers look to data files as a viable answer for storing and retrieving data after the computer's power has been turned off.

Data files are often text based and are used for storing and retrieving related information like that stored in a database. Managing the information contained in data files is up to the C programmer. To help you understand how to manage files, I introduce you to beginning concepts that are used to build files and record layouts for basic data file management.

It's important to understand the breakdown and hierarchy of data files, because each component (parent) and subcomponent (child) are used together to create the whole. Without each component and its hierarchical relationships, building more advanced data file systems such as relational databases would be difficult.

A common data file hierarchy is typically broken down into five categories, as described in Table 11.1.

TABLE 11.1 DATA FILE HIERARCHY

Entity	Description
Bit	Binary digit, 0 or 1
Byte	Eight characters
Field	Grouping of bytes
Record	Grouping of fields
File	Grouping of records

Bits and Bytes

Also known as binary digits, *bits* are the smallest value in a data file. Each bit value can only be a 0 or a 1. Because bits are the smallest unit of measurement in computer systems, they provide an easy mechanism for electrical circuits to duplicate 1s and 0s with patterns of *off* and *on* electrical states. When grouped, bits can build the next unit of data management, known as bytes.

Bytes provide the next step in the data file food chain. They are made up of eight bits and are used to store a single character, such as a number, a letter, or any other character found in a character set. For example, a single byte might contain the letter M, the number 7, or a key-board character such as the exclamation point (!). Together, bytes make up words or, better yet, fields.

Fields, Records, and Files

In database or data-file lingo, groupings of characters are most commonly referred to as *fields*. Fields are often recognized as placeholders in a graphical user interface (GUI) but are really a data concept that groups characters in a range of sizes and data types to provide meaningful information. Fields could be a person's name, social security number, street address, phone number, and so on. For example, the name Sheila could be a value stored in a field called First Name. When combined in a logical group, fields can express a record of information.

Records are logical groupings of fields that comprise a single row of information. Each field in a record describes the record's attributes. For example, a student record might be composed of name, age, ID, major, and GPA fields. Each field is unique in description but together describes a single record.

Individual fields in records are sometimes separated or delimited using spaces, tabs, or commas, as shown in the next sample record that lists field values for a single student:

```
Sheila Vine, 29, 555-55-5555, Computer Science, 4.0
```

Together, records are stored in data files.

Data files are composed of one or more records and are at the top of the data file food chain. Each record in a file typically describes a unique collection of fields. You can use files to store all types of information, such as student or employee data. Data files are normally associated with various database processes in which information can be managed in nonvolatile states, such as a local disk drive, USB flash device, or web server. An example data file called students.dat with comma-delimited records is shown next:

```
Michael Vine, 30, 222-22-2222, Political Science, 3.5
Sheila Vine, 29, 555-55-5555, Computer Science, 4.0
Spencer Vine, 19, 777-77-7777, Law, 3.8
Olivia Vine, 18, 888-88-8888, Medicine, 4.0
```

File Streams

Pointers, pointers, and more pointers! You know you love them, or at least by now you love to hate them. As you may have guessed, anything worth doing in C involves pointers. And, of course, data files are no exception.

C programmers use pointers to manage streams that read and write data. A *stream* is an interface to a disk file or a hardware device, such as a keyboard, monitor, or printer. Although files are clearly different from a hardware device, a stream connects them all, and all can be controlled by C programmers using pointers to the stream.

To point to and manage a file stream in C, simply use an internal data structure called FILE. Pointers of type FILE are created just like any other variable, as the next program demonstrates:

```
#include <stdio.h>
int main()
{
    //create 3 file pointers
    FILE *pRead;
    FILE *pWrite;
    FILE *pAppend;
    return 0;
} //end main
```

As you can see, I created three FILE pointer variables called pRead, pWrite, and pAppend. Using a series of functions that I show you soon, each FILE pointer can open and manage a separate data file.

Opening and Closing Files

The basic components for file processing involve opening, processing, and closing data files. Opening a data file should always involve a bit of error checking or handling. Failure to test the results of a file-open attempt will sometimes cause unwanted program results in your software.

To open a data file, use the standard input/output library function fopen(). The fopen() function is used in an assignment statement to pass a FILE pointer to a previously declared FILE pointer, as the next program reveals:

```
#include <stdio.h>
int main()
{
    FILE *pRead; pRead = fopen("file1.dat", "r");
    return 0;
} //end main
```

This program uses the fopen() function to open a data file, called file1.dat, in a read-only manner (more on this in a moment). The fopen() function returns a FILE pointer to the pRead variable.

DATA FILE EXTENSIONS

It is common to name data files with a .dat extension, although it is not required. Many data files used for processing information have other extensions, such as .txt for text files, .csv for comma separated value files, .ini for initialization files, or .log for log files.

You can create your own data file programs that use file extensions of your choice. For example, I could write my own personal finance software program that opens, reads, and writes to a data file called finance.kpf, in which .kpf stands for Keith's personal finance.

As demonstrated in the previous program, the fopen() function takes two arguments: the first supplies fopen() with the filename to open, and the second argument tells fopen() how to open the file.

Table 11.2 depicts a few common options for opening text files using fopen().

TABLE 11.2 COMMON TEXT FILE OPEN MODES

Mode	Description
r	Opens file for reading
w	Creates file for writing; discards any previous data
a	Writes to end of file (append)

After opening a file, you should always check to ensure that the FILE pointer was returned successfully. In other words, you want to check for occasions when the specified filename cannot be found. Does the Windows error Disk not ready or File not found sound familiar? To test fopen()'s return value, test for a NULL value in a condition, as demonstrated next:

```
#include <stdio.h>

int main()
{
    FILE *pRead;
```

```
    pRead = fopen("file1.dat", "r");
    if ( pRead == NULL )
        printf("\nFile cannot be opened\n");
    else
        printf("\nFile opened for reading\n");
    return 0;
} //end main
```

Trick

The following condition

```
    if ( pRead == NULL )
```

can be shortened with the next condition:

```
    if ( pRead )
```

If pRead **returns a non-NULL, the** if **condition is** true. **If** pRead **returns** NULL, **the condition is** false.

After successfully opening and processing a file, you should close the file using a function called fclose(). The fclose() function uses the FILE pointer to flush the stream and close the file. As shown next, the fclose() function takes a FILE pointer name as an argument:

```
fclose(pRead);
```

In sections to come, I show you more of the fopen() and fclose() functions and how you can use them for managing the reading, writing, and appending of information in data files.

Reading Data

You can easily create your own data files using common text editors such as Vim, nano, or even Microsoft's Notepad. If you're using a Microsoft Windows operating system, you can also use a Microsoft DOS-based system function called copy con, which copies text entered from the keyboard into a predetermined file. The copy con process copies text entered from the console and appends an end-of-file marker using Ctrl+Z, as demonstrated in Figure 11.1.

To read a data file, you need to investigate a few new functions. Specifically, I show you how to read a file's contents and check for the file's EOF (end-of-file) marker using the functions fscanf() and feof().

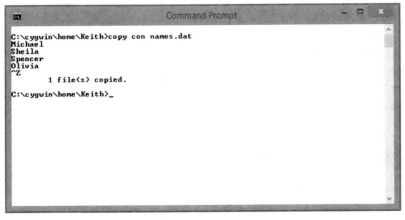

Figure 11.1
Using Microsoft's copy con process to create a data file.

To demonstrate, study the following program that reads a data file called names.dat until an end-of-file marker is read. The output is shown in Figure 11.2:

```c
#include <stdio.h>

int main()
{
    FILE *pRead;
    char name[10];
    pRead = fopen("names.dat", "r");

    if ( pRead == NULL ) {
        printf("\nFile cannot be opened\n");
        return 1; }
    else
        printf("\nContents of names.dat\n\n");
        fscanf(pRead, "%s", name);
        while ( !feof(pRead) ) {
            printf("%s\n", name);
            fscanf(pRead, "%s", name);
        } //end loop
    return 0;
} //end main
```

Trap

If you did not create names.dat using copy con from the command prompt as mentioned previously, the preceding program exits with the error message File cannot be opened and returns 1 to the operating system, indicating an error condition. Additionally, the last record of the file is not read unless there is a carriage return at the end of that line, so be sure to press the Enter key after you enter the last record!

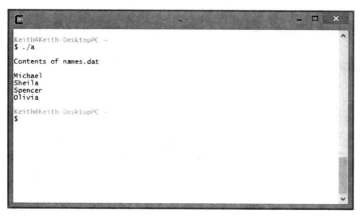

Figure 11.2
Reading information from a data file.

After successfully opening names.dat, I use the fscanf() function to read a single field within the file. The fscanf() function is similar to the scanf() function but works with FILE streams and takes three arguments: a FILE pointer, a data type, and a variable in which to store the retrieved value. After reading the record, I can use the printf() function to display data from the file.

Most data files contain more than one record. To read multiple records, it is common to use a looping structure that can read all records until a condition is met. If you want to read all records until the end-of-file is met, the feof() function provides a nice solution. Using the not operator (!), you can pass the FILE pointer to the feof() function and loop until the function returns a non-zero value when an end-of-file marker is reached.

fscanf() can also read records containing multiple fields by supplying to the second argument a series of type specifiers for each field in the record. For example, the next fscanf() function expects to read two character strings called name and hobby:

```
fscanf(pRead, "%s%s", name, hobby);
```

The %s type specifier reads a series of characters until a white space is found, including blank, new line, or tab.

Other valid type specifiers you can use with the fscanf() function are listed in Table 11.3.

TABLE 11.3 FSCANF() TYPE SPECIFIERS

Type	Description
c	Single character
d	Decimal integer
e, E, f, g, G	Floating point
o	Octal integer
S	String of characters
u	Unsigned decimal integer
x, X	Hexadecimal integer

To demonstrate how a file containing records with multiple fields is read, study the next program and its output in Figure 11.3:

```
#include <stdio.h>

int main()
{
    FILE *pRead;
    char name[10];
    char hobby[15];
    pRead = fopen("hobbies.dat", "r");

    if ( pRead == NULL )
        printf("\nFile cannot be opened\n");
    else
        printf("\nName\tHobby\n\n");
        fscanf(pRead, "%s%s", name, hobby);
        while ( !feof(pRead) ) {
            printf("%s\t%s\n", name, hobby);
            fscanf(pRead, "%s%s", name, hobby);
        } //end loop
    return 0;
} //end main
```

Trap

If you don't have hobbies.dat in the directory with the preceding program, it exits with the error message File cannot be opened and returns a 1 to the operating system, indicating an error condition. To experiment with the program without error, create a text file called hobbies.dat that contains a list of names and hobbies similar to the one shown in Figure 11.3, and save it to the same directory as your test program.

Figure 11.3
Reading records in a data file with multiple fields.

Writing Data

Writing information to a data file is just as easy as reading data. In fact, you can use a function similar to printf() called fprintf() that uses a FILE pointer to write data to a file. The fprintf() function takes a FILE pointer, a list of data types, and a list of values (or variables) to write information to a data file, as demonstrated in the next program and in Figure 11.4:

```c
#include <stdio.h>

int main()
{
    FILE *pWrite;
    char fName[20];
    char lName[20];
    char game[15];
    int score;
    pWrite = fopen("highscore.dat", "w");
```

```
    if ( pWrite == NULL ) {
        printf("\nFile not opened\n");
        return 1; }
    else {
        printf("\nEnter first name, last name, game name, and game score\n\n");
        printf("Enter data separated by spaces: ");
        //store data entered by the user into variables
        scanf("%s%s%s%d", fName, lName, game, &score);
        //write variable contents separated by tabs
        fprintf(pWrite, "%s\t%s\t%s\t%d\n", fName, lName, game, score);
        fclose(pWrite);
    } //end if
    return 0;
} //end main
```

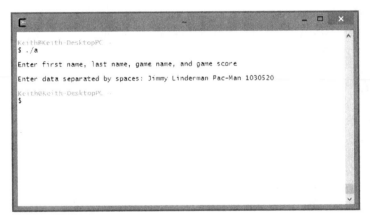

Figure 11.4
Writing a record of information to a data file.

In the preceding program, I ask the user to enter high-score information, including name, game, and high score. Each piece of information is considered a field in the record and is separated during input with a space. In other words, I am able to read an entire line of data using a single scanf() function with the user entering multiple pieces of data separated by spaces. After reading each field of data, I use the fprintf() function to write variables to a data file called highscore.dat. By separating each field in the record with a tab (I've created a tab-delimited file), I can easily read the same record back with the following program:

```
#include <stdio.h>

int main()
{
    FILE *pRead;
    char fName[20];
    char lName[20];
    char game[15];
    int score;
    pRead = fopen("highscore.dat", "r");

    if ( pRead == NULL ) {
        printf("\nFile not opened\n");
        return 1; }
    else {
        //print heading
        printf("\nName\t\tGame\t\tScore\n\n");
        //read field information from data file and store in variables
        fscanf(pRead, "%s%s%s%d", fName, lName, game, &score);
        //print variable data to standard output
        printf("%s %s\t%s\t\t%d\n", fName, lName, game, score);
        fclose(pRead);
    } //end if
    return 0;
} //end main
```

Figure 11.5 shows the output of reading the tab-delimited file created in the preceding code.

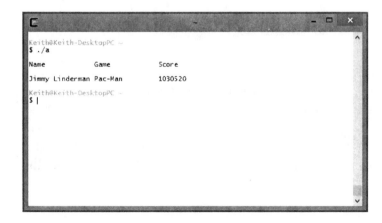

Figure 11.5
Reading information from a data file created by the fprintf() function.

Keep in mind that opening a data file using fopen() with a w argument value erases any previous data stored in the file. Use the a attribute to append data at the end of the file, as discussed in the next section.

Appending Data

Appending data is a common process among information technology (IT) professionals because it enables programmers to continue building upon an existing file without deleting or removing previously stored data.

Appending information to a data file involves opening a data file for writing using the a attribute in an fopen() function and writing records or data to the end of an existing file. If the file does not exist, however, a new data file is created.

Study the following program, which demonstrates appending records to an existing data file:

```c
#include <stdio.h>

void readData(void);

int main()
{
    FILE *pWrite;
    char name[10];
    char hobby[15];

    printf("\nCurrent file contents:\n");
    readData();

      printf("\nEnter a new name and hobby: ");
      scanf("%s%s", name, hobby);

      //open data file for append
      pWrite = fopen("hobbies.dat", "a");

      if ( pWrite == NULL )
          printf("\nFile cannot be opened\n");
      else {
          //append record information to data file
          fprintf(pWrite, "%s %s\n", name, hobby);
          fclose(pWrite);
```

```
        readData();
    } //end if
    return 0;
} //end main

void readData(void)
{
    FILE *pRead;
    char name[10];
    char hobby[15];

    //open data file for read access only
    pRead = fopen("hobbies.dat", "r");

    if ( pRead == NULL )
        printf("\nFile cannot be opened\n");
    else {
        printf("\nName\tHobby\n\n");
        fscanf(pRead, "%s%s", name, hobby);
        //read records from data file until end of file is reached
        while ( !feof(pRead) ) {
            printf("%s\t%s\n", name, hobby);
            fscanf(pRead, "%s%s", name, hobby);
        } //end loop
    } //end if
    fclose(pRead);
} //end readData
```

With a user-defined function called readData(), I'm able to open the hobbies.dat data file created earlier and read each record until the end-of-file is encountered. After the readData() function is finished, I prompt the user to enter another record. After successfully writing the user's new record to the data file, I once again call the readData() function to print again all records, including the one added by the user. Figure 11.6 depicts the process of appending information to data files using the preceding program.

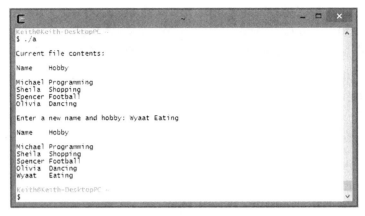

Figure 11.6
Appending records to a data file.

goto and Error Handling

Whenever your program interacts with the outside world, you should provide some form of error handling to counteract unexpected inputs or outputs. One way of providing error handling is to write your own error-handling routines.

Error-handling routines are the traffic control for your program. The best error-handling routines consider a multitude of programming and human-generated error possibilities, resolve issues if possible, and exit the program gracefully after an unresolvable error.

A Brief History of goto

The goto keyword is a carryover from an old programming practice made popular in various languages such as BASIC, COBOL, and even C. A goto was regularly used for designing and building modularized programs. To break programs into manageable pieces, programmers would create modules and link them using the keyword goto in hopes of simulating function calls.

After years of programming with goto, programmers began to realize that this created messy "spaghetti-like" code, which at times became nearly impossible to follow or debug. Fortunately, improvements to the structured programming paradigm and event–driven and object-oriented programming techniques have virtually eliminated the need for goto.

Because of the lack of built-in exception handling within the C language, it is acceptable to use the once infamous goto keyword. Specifically, if you'd like to separate out error handling from each routine and save yourself from writing repetitive error handlers, goto may be a good alternative for you.

Using goto is simple: first include a label (a descriptive name) followed by a colon (:) above where you want your error-handling routine to run (begin). To call your error-handling routine (where you want to check for an error), simply use the keyword goto followed by the label name. Here's an example:

```c
int myFunction()
{
    int iReturnValue = 0; //0 for success
    /* process something */
    if(error)
    {
        goto ErrorHandler; //go to the error-handling routine
    }
    /* do some more processing */
    if(error)
    {
        ret_val = [error];
        goto ErrorHandler; //go to the error-handling routine
    }
ErrorHandler:
    /* error-handling routine */
    return iReturnValue ;
}
```

The label in the preceding code is ErrorHandler, which is simply a name I came up with to identify or label my error handler. In the same sample code, you can see that I want to check for errors in each of the if constructs. If an error exists, I call my error handler using the keyword goto.

Review the next programming example, with output shown in Figure 11.7, that demonstrates the use of goto and a couple of new functions (perror() and exit()) to build error handling into a file I/O program:

```c
#include <stdio.h>
#include <stdlib.h>

int main()
{
    FILE *pRead;
    char name[10];
    char hobby[15];
    pRead = fopen("hobbies.dat", "r");
```

```
    if ( pRead == NULL )
        goto ErrorHandler;
    else {
        printf("\nName\tHobby\n\n");
        fscanf(pRead, "%s%s", name, hobby);
        while ( !feof(pRead) ) {
            printf("%s\t%s\n", name, hobby);
            fscanf(pRead, "%s%s", name, hobby);
        } //end loop
    } //end if

    exit(EXIT_SUCCESS); //exit program normally

    ErrorHandler:
        perror("The following error occurred");
        exit(EXIT_FAILURE); //exit program with error
} //end main
```

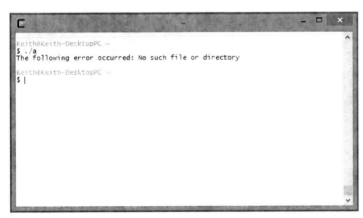

Figure 11.7
Using perror() and exit() functions to display an error message and exit the program.

The exit() function, part of the <stdlib.h> library, terminates a program as if it were exited normally. As shown next, the exit() function is common with programmers who want to terminate a program when encountering file I/O (input/output) errors:

```
exit(EXIT_SUCCESS); //exit program normally
//or
exit(EXIT_FAILURE); //exit program with error
```

The exit() function takes a single parameter, a constant of either EXIT_SUCCESS or EXIT_ FAIL-URE, both of which return a predefined value for success or failure, respectively.

The perror() function sends a message to standard output describing the last error encountered. The perror() function takes a single string argument, which is printed first, followed by a colon and a space, and then the system-generated error message and a new line, as revealed next:

```
perror("The following error occurred");
```

Chapter Program: Character Roster

The Character Roster program shown in Figure 11.8 uses many chapter-based concepts—including fields, records, data files, FILE pointers, and error handling—to build a simple electronic list of game characters. Specifically, the Character Roster program lets a user add characters' first and last names, as well as their achievement level, and list the entire contents of the roster.

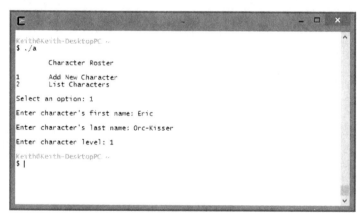

Figure 11.8
Appending records to a data file.

After reading this chapter and studying the code from the Character Roster program, you should be able to build your own programs that use data files to store all kinds of information. In addition, you could build your own database-like program or make modifications to mine, as outlined in the Challenges section.

Here is all the code required to build the Character Roster program:

```
#include <stdio.h>
#include <stdlib.h>

int main() {
```

```c
int response;
char * lName[20] = {0};
char * fName[20] = {0};
char * level[20] = {0};
FILE * pWrite;
FILE * pRead;

printf("\n\tCharacter Roster\n");
printf("\n1\tAdd New Character\n");
printf("2\tList Characters\n\n");
printf("Select an option: ");

scanf("%d", & response);

  if (response == 1) {

      /* user is adding a new character - get the info */
      printf("\nEnter character's first name: ");
      scanf("%s", fName);

      printf("\nEnter character's last name: ");
      scanf("%s", lName);

      printf("\nEnter character level: ");
      scanf("%s", level);

    pWrite = fopen("character_roster.dat", "a");

    if (pWrite != NULL) {
        fprintf(pWrite, "%s %s %s\n", fName, lName, level);
        fclose(pWrite);

    } else goto ErrorHandler; //there is a file i/o error

} else if (response == 2) {

    /* user wants to list all characters */
    pRead = fopen("character_roster.dat", "r");
```

```
        if (pRead != NULL) {
            printf("\nCharacter Roster\n");

            while (!feof(pRead)) {
                fscanf(pRead, "%s %s %s", fName, lName, level);

                if (!feof(pRead))
                    printf("\n%s %s\t%s", fName, lName, level);
            } //end loop

            printf("\n");

        } else goto ErrorHandler; //there is a file i/o error

    } else {
        printf("\nInvalid selection\n");

    }

    exit(EXIT_SUCCESS); //exit program normally

    ErrorHandler: perror("The following error occurred");
    exit(EXIT_FAILURE); //exit program with error

} //end main
```

Summary

- Data files are often text based and are used for storing and retrieving related information like that stored in a database.
- Also known as binary digits, bits are the smallest value in a data file; each bit value can only be a 0 or a 1.
- Bits are the smallest unit of measurement in computer systems.
- Bytes are most commonly made up of eight bits and are used to store a single character, such as a number, a letter, or any other character found in a character set.
- Groupings of characters are referred to as fields.
- Records are logical groupings of fields that comprise a single row of information.

- Data files are composed of one or more records.
- Use an internal data structure called FILE to point to and manage a file stream in C.
- To open a data file, use the standard input/output library function fopen().
- The fclose() function uses the FILE pointer to flush the stream and close the file.
- The fscanf() function is similar to the scanf() function but works with FILE streams and takes three arguments: a FILE pointer, a data type, and a variable in which to store the retrieved value.
- To test when an end-of-file marker is reached, pass the FILE pointer to the feof() function and loop until the function returns a non-zero value.
- The fprintf() function takes a FILE pointer, a list of data types, and a list of values (or variables) to write information to a data file.
- Appending information to a data file involves opening a data file for writing using the a attribute in an fopen() function and writing records or data to the end of an existing file.
- The keyword goto is used to simulate function calls and can be leveraged to build error-handling routines.
- The exit() function terminates a program.
- The perror() function sends a message to standard output describing the last error encountered.

Challenges

1. Create a data file called superheroes.dat using any text-based editor, and enter at least three records storing superheroes' names and main superpower. Make sure that each field in the record is separated by a space.

2. Using the superheroes.dat file from Challenge 1, build another program that uses the fscanf() function for reading each record and printing field information to standard output until the end-of-file is reached. Include an error-handling routine that notifies the user of any system errors and exits the program.

3. Create a program that uses a menu with options to enter information about monsters (monster type, special ability, weakness), print the monster information, or quit the program. Use data files and FILE pointers to store and print information entered.

4. Modify the Character Roster program to enable the user to enter multiple entries without quitting and restarting the program.

5. Continue to modify the Character Roster program to enable a user to modify or delete the characters and their levels in the roster.

12

The C Preprocessor

Understanding the C preprocessor is an important step in learning how to build large programs with multiple files. In this chapter, you learn how to break your C programs into separate files and use the gcc compiler to link and compile those files into a single working executable software program. Moreover, you learn about preprocessor techniques and concepts such as symbolic constants, macros, function headers, and definition files.

Specifically, this chapter covers the following topics:

- Understanding the C preprocessor
- Building larger programs
- Chapter program: the Function Wizard

Understanding the C Preprocessor

C programs must go through a number of steps before an executable file can be created. The most common of these steps are performed by the preprocessor, compiler, and linker, which are orchestrated by software programs such as gcc. As discussed in Chapter 1, "Getting Started with C Programming," the gcc program performs the following actions to create an executable file:

1. Preprocesses program code and looks for various directives
2. Generates error codes and messages
3. Compiles program code into object code and stores it temporarily on disk
4. Links any necessary library to the object code and creates an executable file stored on disk

In this chapter, I concentrate primarily on preprocessing, which generally involves reading specialized statements called *preprocessor directives*. Preprocessor directives are often found littered through C source files (source files end with a .c extension) and can serve many common and useful functions. Specifically, ANSI C preprocessors, such as the one found in gcc, can insert or replace text and organize source code through conditional compilation. The type of preprocessor directive encountered dictates each of these functions.

You have already been using preprocessor directives since your first program. Consider the C library header files <stdio.h> and <string.h>, which commonly appear at the beginning of C programs. To use library functions defined in header files, such as printf() or scanf(), you must tell the C preprocessor to include the specific header file or files using a preprocessor directive called #include.

Here's a simple program that uses this preprocessor directive:

```c
#include <stdio.h>

int main()
{
    printf("\nHaving fun with preprocessor directives\n");
    return 0;
}
```

The pound (#) sign is a special preprocessor character that is used to direct the preprocessor to perform some action. In fact, all preprocessor directives are prefaced with the # symbol. Moreover, you might be surprised to learn that the preprocessor has its own language that can be used to build symbolic constants and macros.

Symbolic Constants

Symbolic constants are easy to understand. In fact, symbolic constants are similar in application to the constant data type you learned about in Chapter 2, "Primary Data Types." Like other preprocessor directives, symbolic constants must be created outside of any function.

In addition, symbolic constants must be preceded by a #define preprocessor directive, as shown next:

```
#define NUMBER 7
```

When the preprocessor encounters a symbolic constant name, in this case NUMBER, it replaces all occurrences of the constant name found in the source code with its definition, in this case 7. Remember, this is a preprocessor directive, so the process of text replacement occurs before your program is compiled into an executable file. Refer to the following program and its output in Figure 12.1 for an example of how symbolic constants work:

```
#include <stdio.h>
#define NUMBER 7

int main()
{
    printf("\nLucky Number %d\n", NUMBER);
    return 0;

}
```

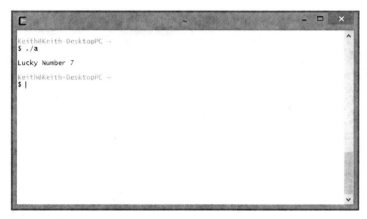

Figure 12.1
Demonstrating preprocessor directives using symbolic constants.

You should follow two rules when working with symbolic constants. First, always capitalize symbolic constants so that they are easy to spot in your program code. Second, do not attempt to reassign data to symbolic constants, as demonstrated next:

```c
#include <stdio.h>
#define NUMBER 7

int main()
{
    printf("\nLucky Number %d\n", NUMBER);
    NUMBER = 5; //cannot do this
    return 0;
}
```

Attempting to change a symbolic constant's value will prevent your program from successfully compiling, as Figure 12.2 reveals.

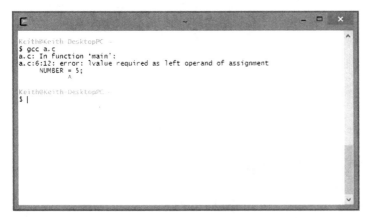

Figure 12.2
Attempting to change the value of a symbolic constant generates a compiler error.

ARE PREPROCESSOR DIRECTIVES C STATEMENTS?

Preprocessor directives are actions performed before the compiler begins its job. Preprocessor directives act only to change the source program before the source code is compiled. The reason semicolons are not used is because they are not C statements, and they are not executed during a program's execution. In the case of #include, the preprocessor directive expands the source code so the compiler sees a much larger source program when it finally gets to do its job.

Creating and Using Macros

Macros provide another interesting investigation into preprocessor text replacement. In fact, C preprocessors treat macros similarly to symbolic constants—they use text-replacement techniques and are created with the #define statement.

Macros provide a useful shortcut to tasks that are performed frequently. For example, consider the following formula that computes the area of a rectangle:

```
Area of a rectangle = length x width
```

If the area values of length and width were always 10 and 5, you could build a macro like this:

```
#define AREA 10 * 5
```

In the real world, however, you know that this would be very limiting, if not useless. Macros can play a greater role when they're built to use incoming and outgoing variables like a user-defined function would. When built in this way, macros can save a C programmer keyboard time when using easily repeated statements. To demonstrate, study the next program that improves the area of a rectangle formula:

```c
#include <stdio.h>
#define AREA(l,w) ( l * w )

int main()
{
    int length = 0;
    int width = 0;

    printf("\nEnter length: ");
    scanf("%d", &length);

    printf("\nEnter width: ");
    scanf("%d", &width);

    printf("\nArea of rectangle = %d\n", AREA(length,width));
    return 0;

}
```

Figure 12.3 demonstrates a sample output from the preceding program, which uses a macro to determine the area of a rectangle.

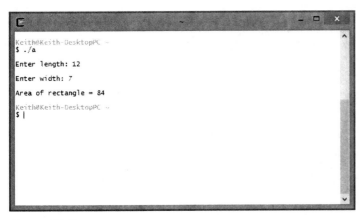

Figure 12.3
Using a macro to calculate the area of a rectangle.

As you can see in Figure 12.3, the macro acts similarly to any C library or user-defined function—it takes arguments and returns values. The C preprocessor has replaced the reference of the AREA macro inside the main() function with the macro definition defined outside of the main() function. Once again, all this happens prior to compiling (creating) an executable file.

Take a closer look at the macro definition again:

```
#define AREA(l,w) ( l * w )
```

The first part of this macro defines its name, AREA. The next sequence of characters (l,w) tells the preprocessor that this macro will receive two arguments. The last part of the AREA macro (l * w) explains to the preprocessor what the macro will do. The preprocessor does not perform the macro's calculation. Instead, it replaces any reference to the name AREA in source files with the macro's definition.

You may be surprised to find out that besides simple numerical computation, macros can contain library functions such as printf(), as shown in the next program (with output shown in Figure 12.4):

```
#include <stdio.h>
#define RESULT(x,y) ( printf("\nResult is %d\n", x+y) )

int main()
{
    int num1 = 0;
    int num2 = 0;
```

```
    printf("\nEnter first number: ");
    scanf("%d", & num1);

    printf("\nEnter second number: ");
    scanf("%d", & num2);

    RESULT(num1, num2);
    return 0;
}
```

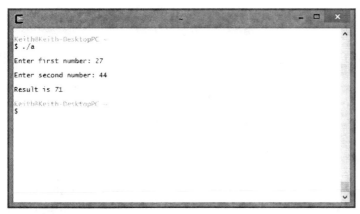

Figure 12.4
Using the printf() function inside a macro definition.

Figure 12.4 demonstrates that you can easily use library functions inside macro definitions. Remember: do not use a semicolon in the macro definition. Take another look at the macro definition I used:

```
#define RESULT(x,y) ( printf("\nResult is %d\n", x+y) )
```

I didn't use a semicolon to end the statement within the macro definition or to end the macro itself because the gcc compiler would have returned a parse error, which happens to be at the line number at which I reference the RESULT macro. But why at the line where I reference the macro and not the line at which the macro is defined? Remember, the preprocessor replaces text with references to #define preprocessor directives; when it attempts to replace the RESULT reference, the source code for the main() function might look something like this:

```
int main()
{
    int operand1 = 0;
    int operand2 = 0;
```

```
    printf("\nEnter first operand: ");
    scanf("%d", &operand1);

    printf("\nEnter second operand: ");
    scanf("%d", &operand2);

    /* The following macro reference... */
    RESULT(num1, num2);
    /* ...might be replaced with this: */
    printf("\nResult is %d\n", x+y);; //notice the extra semicolon
    return 0;
}
```

Notice the extra semicolon in the last `printf()` function. Because a semicolon was used in the macro definition and in the macro call, two semicolons were processed by the compiler, potentially creating a parse error.

Building Larger Programs

In Chapter 5, "Structured Programming," I touched on the concept of breaking large problems into smaller, more manageable ones using structured programming techniques such as top-down design and functions. In this section, I will show you how you can extend those concepts by splitting your programs into separate program files using preprocessor directives, header files, and gcc.

Dividing a program into separate files enables you to easily reuse your components (functions) and provides an environment in which multiple programmers can work simultaneously on the same software application. You already know that structured programming involves breaking problems into manageable components. So far, you have learned how to do so by dividing your tasks into components that are built with function prototypes and headers. With this knowledge and the understanding of how the C preprocessor works with multiple files, you will find it easy to divide your programs into separate file entities.

Consider the preprocessor directive `#include <stdio.h>`. This directive tells the C preprocessor to include the standard input output library with your program during the linking process. Moreover, the `<stdio.h>` library consists primarily of function headers or prototypes—thus the `.h` extension. The actual function implementations or definitions for the standard input output library are stored in a completely different file called `stdio.c`. You don't have to include this file in your programs because the gcc compiler automatically knows where to find it based on the associated header file and predefined directory structure.

You can easily build your own header and definition files using your knowledge of functions and a few new techniques. To prove this, consider a simple program that calculates a profit. To calculate a profit, use the following equation:

```
Profit = (price)(quantity sold) — total cost
```

I will break down a program to calculate a profit into three separate files:

- **Function header file**—profit.h
- **Function definition file**—profit.c
- **Main function**—main.c

Header Files

Header files end with an .h extension and contain function prototypes including various data types or constants required by the functions. To build the function header file for my profit program, I'll create a new file called profit.h and place the following function prototype in it:

```
void profit(float, float, float);
```

Because I'm using a single user-defined function in my profit program, the preceding statement is the only code required in my header file. I could have created this file in any text editing program such as vi, nano, or Microsoft Notepad.

Function Definition File

Function definition files contain all the code required to implement function prototypes found in corresponding header files. After building my header file with the required function prototype, I can begin work on creating its corresponding function definition file, which is called profit.c.

For the profit program, my function implementation looks like the following:

```
#include <stdio.h>

void profit(float p, float q, float tc)
{
    printf("\nYour profit is %.2f\n", (p * q) - tc);
}
```

At this point, I've created two separate files: profit.h for my function prototype and profit.c for my function implementation. Keep in mind that neither of these files has been compiled. More on this in a moment.

main() Function File

Now that I've built both function header and definition files, I can concentrate on creating my main program file, where I will pull everything together with the help of the C preprocessor. All the code required to build the profit program's main() function is revealed next:

```c
#include <stdio.h>
#include "profit.h"

int main()
{
    float price, totalCost;
    int quantity;

    printf("\nThe Profit Program\n");
    printf("\nEnter unit price: ");
    scanf("%f", &price);

    printf("Enter quantity sold: ");
    scanf("%d", &quantity);

    printf("Enter total cost: ");
    scanf("%f", &totalCost);

    profit(price,quantity,totalCost);
    return 0;
} //end main
```

All the program code stored in main.c is pretty straightforward and should be familiar to you, with one exception shown next:

```c
#include <stdio.h> #include "profit.h"
```

The first preprocessor directive tells the C preprocessor to find and include the standard input output library header file. Surrounding a header file in an #include statement with the less than (<) and greater than (>) symbols tells the C preprocessor to look in a predefined installation directory. The second #include statement also tells the C preprocessor to include a header file; this time, however, I've used double quotes to surround my own header filename. Using double quotes in this fashion tells the C preprocessor to look for the header file in the same directory as the file being compiled.

To properly link and compile a program that uses multiple files, pass all definition files ending in .c, separated by a space, to the gcc compiler, as demonstrated in Figure 12.5.

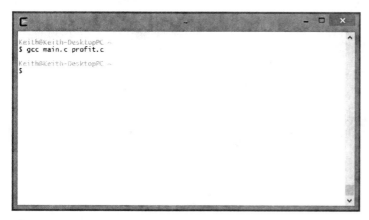

Figure 12.5
Using gcc to link multiple files.

After preprocessing directives, linking multiple files, and compiling, gcc produces a single working executable file demonstrated in Figure 12.6.

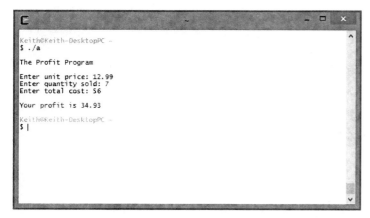

Figure 12.6
Demonstrating the output of a program built with multiple files.

Chapter Program: The Function Wizard

Shown in Figure 12.7, the Function Wizard uses multiple files to build a single program that calculates the following rectangle-based functions:

- Determine perimeter of a rectangle
- Determine area of a rectangle
- Determine volume of a rectangle

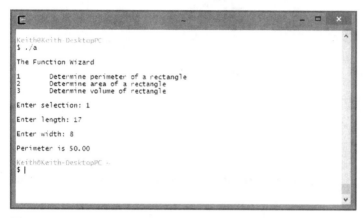

Figure 12.7
Using chapter-based concepts to build the Function Wizard program.

All program code for each file in the Function Wizard is listed next in its appropriate section.

ch12_calculate.h

The header file `ch12_calculate.h` lists three function prototypes that calculate the perimeter, area, and volume of a rectangle:

```
void perimeter(float, float);
void area(float, float);
void volume(float, float, float);
```

ch12_calculate.c

The function definition file `ch12_calculate.c` implements the three rectangle functions prototyped in `ch12_calculate.h`:

```
#include <stdio.h>
void perimeter(float l, float w)
```

```
{
    printf("\nPerimeter is %.2f\n", (2*l) + (2*w));
}

void area(float l, float w)
{
    printf("\nArea is %.2f\n", l * w);
}

void volume(float l, float w, float h)
{
    printf("\nThe volume is %.2f\n", l * w * h);
}
```

ch12_main.c

The main program file ch12_main.c enables the user to calculate the perimeter, area, and volume of a rectangle. Notice the inclusion of the header file ch12_header.h, which contains the rectangle-based function prototypes:

```
#include <stdio.h>
#include "ch12_calculate.h"

int main()
{
    int selection = 0;
    float l,w,h;

    printf("\nThe Function Wizard\n");
    printf("\n1\tDetermine perimeter of a rectangle\n");
    printf("2\tDetermine area of a rectangle\n");
    printf("3\tDetermine volume of rectangle\n");

    printf("\nEnter selection: ");
    scanf("%d", &selection);

    switch (selection) {
    case 1:
        printf("\nEnter length: ");
        scanf("%f", &l);
```

```
        printf("\nEnter width: ");
        scanf("%f", &w);
        perimeter(l,w);
        break;
    case 2:
        printf("\nEnter length: ");
        scanf("%f", &l);
        printf("\nEnter width: ");
        scanf("%f", &w);
        area(l,w);
        break;
    case 3:
        printf("\nEnter length: ");
        scanf("%f", &l);
        printf("\nEnter width: ");
        scanf("%f", &w);
        printf("\nEnter height: ");
        scanf("%f", &h);
        volume(l,w,h);
        break;
    } // end switch
    return 0;
} // end main
```

Remember to compile both source files, as follows:

```
$ gcc ch12_main.c ch12_calculate.c
```

Summary

- The pound (#) sign is a special preprocessor character that directs the preprocessor to perform some action.
- Symbolic constants must be created outside of any function and must be preceded by a #define preprocessor directive.
- Attempting to change a symbolic constant's value will prevent your program from successfully compiling.

- Preprocessor directives are not implemented with C syntax and, therefore, do not require the use of a semicolon after program statements. Inserting a semicolon at the end of a preprocessor directive will cause a parse error during compilation.
- Macros provide a useful shortcut to tasks that are performed frequently.
- Macros can contain library functions such as `printf()`.
- Dividing a program into separate files allows you to easily reuse your components (functions) and provides an environment in which multiple programmers can work simultaneously on the same software application.
- Header files end with an `.h` extension and contain function prototypes including various data types or constants that the functions require.
- Function definition files contain all the code required to implement function prototypes found in corresponding header files.
- Using double quotes to surround a header filename tells the C preprocessor to look for the header file in the same directory as the file being compiled.
- Pass all definition files ending in `.c`, separated by a space, to the gcc compiler to properly link and compile a program that uses multiple files.

Challenges

1. Build a program that creates a macro to calculate the area of a circle using the formula

   Area = π • r² (area = pi × radius × radius)

   In the same program, prompt the user to enter a circle's radius. Use the macro to calculate the circle's area and display the result to the user.

2. Build a simple program that prompts a user to input the length and width of a rectangle using a macro to calculate the perimeter. After retrieving the length and width, pass the data as arguments in a call to the macro. Use the following algorithm to derive the perimeter of a rectangle:

   Perimeter of a rectangle = 2(length) + 2 (width)

3. Use a similar program design as in Challenge 1 that uses a macro to calculate the total revenue. Use the following formula to calculate the total revenue:

   Total revenue = (price)(quantity)

4. Modify the Function Wizard program to include the following function:

   Average cost = total cost / quantity

5. Divide the Cryptogram program from Chapter 7, "Pointers," into multiple files using chapter-based concepts.

What's Next?

C is not an easy programming language to learn, so you should feel a sense of accomplishment in learning what is considered one of the most challenging and powerful programming languages ever developed.

If you haven't done so already, create programs to solve the challenges at the end of each chapter. I can't emphasize enough that the only way to learn how to program is to program. It's just like learning a spoken language; you can get only so much from reading and listening. Speaking a language regularly is the key to learning it and, in this case, programming is the key to learning the C language.

If you're still hungry for more C, I recommend reviewing Appendix F, "Common C Library Functions." There you will find a number of useful functions to explore. If you are seeking advanced challenges with C, I recommend studying advanced data structures such as linked lists, stacks, queues, and trees.

Another natural progression for C programming students is learning how to develop graphical user interfaces (GUIs) for a Windows-like environment. In today's world, GUIs are often built using object-oriented programming languages with syntax similar to that of C, such as C++, C#, or even Java, all of which require a study of the object-oriented programming (OOP) paradigm.

You can find a wealth of information about these topics and more by searching the Internet or visiting the Cengage Learning website at www.cengageptr.com for more great programming books. Good luck, best wishes, and keep programming!

—Michael Vine and Keith Davenport

Common UNIX Commands

This appendix contains a short list of commonly used UNIX shell commands. For more details on using any of the commands, including their options, enter one of the following commands at a shell prompt:

man *<command>*

or

help *<command>*

For example, to see options for using mkdir to create a new directory, enter the following:

man mkdir

The shell opens the documentation for mkdir. You can press Enter or use the arrow keys to scroll the contents, and when finished, press Q to quit.

Trick

Some commands have full documentation and some don't, so if you don't get the information you need using man *<command>*, try help *<command>*. Note that some commands even use info *<command>* instead.

TABLE A.1 COMMON UNIX COMMANDS

Command Name	Functionality
>	Redirection operator—writes data to a file.
>>	Append operator—appends data to a file.
help	Displays help information for some shell commands.
cat <textfile>	Lists the contents of the specified text file.
cd <directory>	Change to *directory*. If none specified, returns to home directory.
chmod <options> <filename>	Changes file attributes, which determine access permissions.
cp <srcfile> <desfile>	Copies source file to destination file.
date	Displays current date and time of day.
gcc <source filename>	Compiles a C program.
grep <string> <filename>	Searches files for a certain string.
history	Shows previously used shell commands.
kill <options>	Terminates a process.
logout	Exits the console session.
ls	Lists the contents of a directory.
man <command>	Displays documentation (manual) for some shell commands.
mkdir	Creates a directory.
mv <oldname> <newname>	Moves or renames files.
nano <filename>	Edits the specified file in the nano text editor. If no filename is specified, starts the nano editor with an empty file.
ps	Displays process status.
pwd	Displays working directory.
rm	Removes files.
rmdir	Removes a directory.
vim <filename>	Edits the specified file in the Vim text editor. If no filename is specified, starts the Vim editor with an empty file.

Vim Quick Guide

Vim is an improved version of the popular UNIX text editor vi (pronounced "vee-eye"). For the most part, commands found in vi are available in Vim and vice versa.

Using the escape (Esc) key to switch between modes, Vim operates in two distinct forms: insert and command mode. In insert mode, you type characters to construct a document or program. Command mode, however, takes keys pressed and translates them into various functions. The most common frustration of new Vim users is the distinction between these two modes.

Trap

If you don't have Vim installed, rerun the Cygwin setup program. At the Select Packages section, expand the Editors category and select vim and vim-common from the list, which updates your Cygwin installation to make Vim available.

To start Vim, enter vi or vim from the command prompt. Figure B.1 depicts the opening Vim screen.

```
              VIM - Vi IMproved

                version 7.4.316
             by Bram Moolenaar et al.
      Vim is open source and freely distributable

              Sponsor Vim development!
      type  :help sponsor<Enter>    for information

      type  :q<Enter>               to exit
      type  :help<Enter>  or  <F1>  for on-line help
      type  :help version7<Enter>   for version info

             Running in Vi compatible mode
      type  :set nocp<Enter>         for Vim defaults
      type  :help cp-default<Enter> for info on this
```

Figure B.1
The opening Vim screen.

Vim contains a good user's guide and help system, so without reinventing the wheel, I'll show you how to navigate through the built-in Vim help files and user guides.

From within the Vim screen, type the following:

`:help`

The colon in front of the word `help` is required; essentially, it tells Vim that you're entering a command.

As shown in Figure B.2, you can use the arrow keys to navigate through the help file. After viewing the help file, you may notice a list of other files for viewing. You might want to open a second Cygwin shell and start another Vim session so that you can practice along with the Vim user's guide.

```
"help.txt"      For Vim version 7.4.  Last change: 2012 Dec 06

                    VIM - main help file
                                                      k
   Move around:  Use the cursor keys, or "h" to go left,      h   l
                 "j" to go down, "k" to go up, "l" to go right.   j
Close this window:  Use ":q<Enter>".
   Get out of Vim:  Use ":qa!<Enter>" (careful, all changes are lost!).

Jump to a subject:  Position the cursor on a tag (e.g. |bars|) and hit CTRL-].
   With the mouse:  ":set mouse=a" to enable the mouse (in xterm or GUI).
                    Double-click the left mouse button on a tag, e.g. |bars|.
      Jump back:  Type CTRL-T or CTRL-O (repeat to go further back).

Get specific help:  It is possible to go directly to whatever you want help
                    on, by giving an argument to the |:help| command.
                    It is possible to further specify the context:
                                                  *help-context*
                        WHAT              PREPEND    EXAMPLE
                    Normal mode command   (nothing)  :help x
help.txt [Help][RO]

[No Name]
"help.txt" [readonly] 221 lines, 8249 characters
```

Figure B.2
The Vim help screen.

There are ten chapters available in the help file, but I recommend that you view and work through the following files at a minimum:

- `usr_01.txt`
- `usr_02.txt`
- `usr_03.txt`
- `usr_04.txt`

When you're ready to start viewing the next file (`usr_01.txt`), simply type the following from the help screen:

`:help usr_01.txt`

From each of the user document screens, follow the aforementioned pattern to gain access to the next user document.

nano Quick Guide

A free UNIX-based text editor, nano is similar to its less versatile cousin Pico. nano is an easy-to-use and easy-to-learn UNIX text editor with which you can write text files and programs in languages such as Java, C++, and, of course, C.

To start a nano process, simply type the word nano at your Cygwin UNIX command prompt (see Figure C.1). If you're using another UNIX shell other than Cygwin, you may not have access to nano. In this case, you can use the common UNIX editor Pico, which shares many of nano's capabilities and command structures.

Trap

If you don't have nano installed, rerun the Cygwin setup program. At the Select Packages section, expand the Editors category and select nano from the list, which updates your Cygwin installation to make the nano editor available.

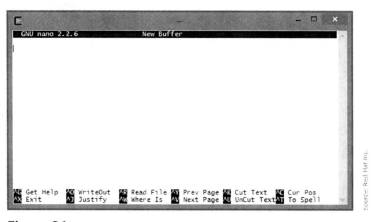

Figure C.1
The free nano UNIX text editor.

Unlike Vim or vi, nano operates under one mode. Its single base mode of operation makes it an excellent candidate for beginning UNIX users but prevents the existence of many advanced text-editing features found in Vim or vi.

To create a new text file (C program, letter, memo, and so on), simply start typing from nano's interface.

nano has two categories of program options. The first category of options is used when you launch the nano program. For example, the following code launches nano with an option to constantly show the cursor position:

```
$ nano c
```

Table C.1 shows a comprehensive list of nano start options. This list is derived from the free nano help file, which you can read in full by entering man nano at the command prompt.

TABLE C.1 NANO START OPTIONS

Option	Description
-T	Sets tab width
-R	Enables regular expression matching for search strings
-V	Shows current version and author
-h	Displays command-line options
-c	Constantly shows the cursor position
-i	Indents new lines to the previous line's indentation
-k	Enables cut from cursor to end of line with Ctrl+K
-l	Replaces symbolic link with a new file
-m	Enables mouse support if available
-p	Emulates Pico
-r	Wraps lines at column number
-s	Enables alternative spell checker command
-t	Saves changed buffer without prompting
-v	Views file in read-only mode
-w	Disables wrapping of long lines
-x	Disables help screen at bottom of editor
-z	Enables suspend ability
+LINE	Places cursor at LINE on startup

Once inside the nano editor, you can use a number of commands to help you edit your text file. You can access most of nano's command structures by using Ctrl-key sequences denoted by the carrot character (^), function keys, or meta keys (Esc or Alt keys). Table C.2 describes the most common nano commands as found in the Get Help feature.

TABLE C.2 COMMON NANO COMMANDS

Ctrl-Key Sequence	Optional Key	Description
^G	F1	Invokes help menu
^X	F2	Exits nano
^O	F3	Writes current file to disk (save)
^R	F5	Inserts new file into the current one
^\		Replaces text within the editor
^W	F6	Searches for text
^Y	F7	Moves to previous screen
^V	F8	Moves to next screen
^K	F9	Cuts current line and stores in buffer
^U	F10	Uncuts from buffer into current line
^C	F11	Shows cursor position
^T	F12	Invokes spell checker if available
^P		Moves to previous line
^N		Moves to next line
^F		Moves forward one character
^B		Moves back one character
^A		Moves to beginning of current line
^E		Moves to end of current line
^L		Refreshes screen
^^		Marks text at current cursor location
^D		Deletes character under cursor
^H		Deletes character to left of cursor
^I		Inserts tab character
^J	F4	Justifies current paragraph
^M		Inserts carriage return at cursor

TCC Quick Guide

The Tiny C Compiler (TCC) is a free C compiler for Windows. TCC was developed by Fabrice Bellard in 2002. Although TCC is no longer being developed, it is still in use by many people and is quite useful for compiling C source code in the Windows environment.

TCC has a few advantages over other C compilers: it is small, fast, and doesn't require any special configuration. Although you probably won't see any difference with the small programs used in this book, TCC produces executable files for Windows several times faster than gcc.

Installing and Configuring TCC for Windows

Downloading, installing, and configuring TCC is similar to installing other programs that run from the Windows command shell, but in case you're not familiar with working with the command prompt in Windows, you can follow the instructions in this and the following sections to prepare TCC to be used with the book's example code.

Downloading TCC

To download TCC, go to http://bellard.org/tcc/ and click on the Download link on that page. The Download link takes you to a page similar to the one shown in Figure D.1.

Index of /releases/tinycc

Name	Last modified	Size	Description
Parent Directory			
tcc-0.9.24-win32-bin.zip	31-Mar-2008 20:54	274K	
tcc-0.9.24.tar.bz2	31-Mar-2008 20:52	356K	
tcc-0.9.25-win32-bin.zip	18-May-2009 13:14	280K	
tcc-0.9.25.tar.bz2	18-May-2009 13:27	374K	
tcc-0.9.26-win32-bin.zip	15-Feb-2013 15:22	386K	
tcc-0.9.26-win64-bin.zip	15-Feb-2013 15:24	389K	
tcc-0.9.26.tar.bz2	15-Feb-2013 15:11	514K	
tcc-0.9.26.tar.bz2.checksums	16-Feb-2013 10:46	158	
tcc-0.9.26.tar.bz2.sig	16-Feb-2013 10:45	543	

Downloads will redirect to your nearest mirror site.
Files on mirrors may be subject to a replication delay of up to 24 hours.
In case of problems use http://download-mirror.savannah.gnu.org/releases/

Source: Fabrice Bellard.

Figure D.1
Choosing the correct distribution of TCC.

If you have a 32-bit version of Windows, click the following link:

```
tcc-0.9.26-win32-bin.zip
```

If you have a 64-bit version of Windows, click this link:

```
tcc-0.9.26-win64-bin.zip
```

Trick

If you don't know if you have a 32-bit or 64-bit version of Windows, go to the Control Panel and double-click the System icon. In the System section, or under the General tab (depending on your version of Windows), it will show the system type as 32-bit or 64-bit.

Download the correct version of TCC for your operating system and save it to your Download folder or another directory of your choice. Because TCC comes in a zip archive, a common archive format, you can open it with Windows Explorer, File Explorer, or a third-party archive utility such as 7-Zip, WinZip, or WinRAR.

Installing TCC

Extract the files for your version of TCC to your hard drive—somewhere easily accessible from the command prompt. I recommend extracting TCC to the root directory of your hard drive (C:\), which creates a folder called tcc and copies the necessary files into that folder.

Trap

Be sure to extract the *entire* contents of the archive to your C:\ drive, not just the files contained in the tcc folder of the archive. You want all the TCC files to end up in the tcc folder on your hard drive, not cluttering your drive's root directory!

Once you have extracted the TCC compiler files, open the command prompt and navigate to the tcc directory.

Trick

To open a command prompt in Windows Vista or Windows 7, click the Start button, navigate to All Programs, Accessories, and click Command Prompt.

To open a command prompt in Windows 8 (or 8.1), type cmd from the Start screen interface, which causes the search menu to appear and populate with Command Prompt, which you can left-click to open the command prompt.

Once you are at the command prompt, change to the tcc folder by entering cd \tcc, as shown in the following example:

```
C:\>cd \tcc
```

Your command prompt should now look like this:

```
C:\tcc>
```

Once you're in the tcc folder, create a subdirectory under that folder in which to keep the code you create using this book. Use the md (make directory) command to create a directory called cbook (or another name of your choosing). Once you have created the directory, list the contents of the tcc directory using the dir (directory) command to confirm the new folder has been created correctly:

```
C:\tcc>md cbook
C:\tcc>dir
```

The output from the two preceding commands is shown in Figure D.2.

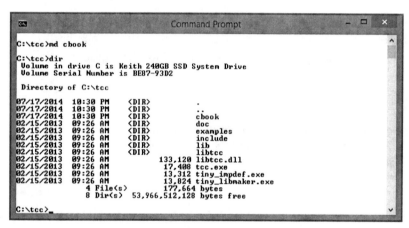

Figure D.2
Creating a working directory for C programs.

Configuring TCC

The only configuration required is to add TCC to the Windows PATH environment variable so Windows can find tcc.exe and its supporting files from anywhere you choose to work.

There are a couple ways to add a program to the Windows PATH, but because we are working with the command prompt anyway, we'll use the command shell to update the PATH. To do so, type the following at the C:\ prompt, and press Enter:

```
set PATH=%PATH%;c:\tcc
```

The preceding command appends c:\tcc to the end of the current PATH variable, meaning that it adds c:\tcc to the end of the current path instead of overwriting the PATH, which would be bad. To verify the command was successful, type the keyword PATH alone from the command prompt and press Enter. You should see the entire PATH variable contents with c:\tcc appended to the end.

Creating, Compiling, and Executing Code

Creating C programs—from text file to executable file using TCC and Notepad—is straightforward. I'll walk you through the creation of the C You Later, World program from Chapter 1 to ensure you're comfortable with the process of creating, compiling, and executing C code using Windows Notepad and TCC.

Creating and Editing Source Code

You can use Windows Notepad or any plain-text editor to create and edit source code that will be compiled or recompiled with TCC. For this example, open Notepad and enter the following code:

```
/* C Programming for the Absolute Beginner */
//by Your Name

#include <stdio.h>

int main()
{
    printf("\nC you later\n");
    return 0;
}
```

When you're finished entering the source code, save the file as cya.c to the cbook folder (or whatever you called your example code folder from the earlier "Installing TCC" section), as shown in Figure D.3.

Trick

Don't worry if you have not yet started working through the book and don't understand the code you're entering. The example here is to teach you the *process* of using TCC and Notepad to take you from creating a source code text file to running an executable C program.

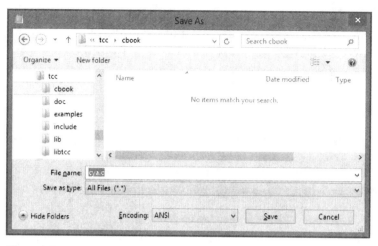

Figure D.3
Saving cya.c to your source code folder.

Once your `cya.c` file is saved to the `cbook` directory under the `tcc` folder, you can compile and execute `cya.c`.

Compiling and Executing Source Code

Using TCC to compile and execute the source code you created in Notepad is easy once you have TCC installed and configured.

If you are not already at the command prompt, start it and navigate to the `cbook` folder by entering `cd \tcc\cbook` (and pressing Enter):

```
C:\cd \tcc\cbook
```

Once you are in the `cbook` subdirectory, enter the `dir` command to ensure your `cya.c` file is present. If it's not, go back and save the file again, ensuring that you save it to the correct folder.

To compile `cya.c` into an executable file, enter `tcc cya.c` at the command prompt and press Enter, as shown here:

```
C:\tcc\cbook>tcc cya.c
```

For most of the examples in the book, the preceding is all you'll need to do to compile your source code.

Trick

When working with more than once source file, which is something you do in more advanced programming (and in Chapter 12 of this book, "The C Preprocessor"), you need to combine two source files into a single executable file. The easiest way to accomplish this in TCC is to simply add the second source file after the first and a space, as shown here:

```
C:\tcc\cbook>tcc source1.c source2.c
```

The preceding combines the source1.c and source2.c files into a single executable file called source1.exe.

Enter the dir command at the C:\tcc\cbook> prompt, and you will see (assuming you didn't make any typing errors) a new file in the directory called cya.exe. To execute your new cya.exe program, enter cya (or cya.exe) at the command prompt.

The results of using the dir command, followed by the result of executing cya.exe, are shown in Figure D.4.

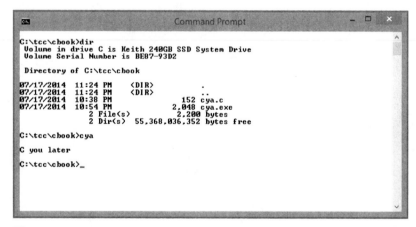

Figure D.4
Listing and executing cya.exe.

There are many other options for compiling source code with TCC, which you can read about in the official documentation. The HTML version of the TCC documentation is called tcc-doc.html and is found in the doc subdirectory under the tcc directory. If you double-click tcc-doc.html from within Windows Explorer or File Explorer, the Tiny C Compiler Reference Documentation file opens in your default browser.

ASCII Character Codes

ASCII stands for American Standard Code for Information Interchange. Because computers can, ultimately, only understand numbers, programmers use ASCII as a numerical representation of standard and special characters.

ASCII was developed before the advent of computers (for use with teletype machines), so some of the descriptions are outdated. The first 31 codes, called *control codes*, are rarely used for their original intent. Codes 32–127 are printable characters.

Hint

Some companies added additional ASCII codes beyond the 127 to support special symbols. For example, many software programs use the extended ASCII table known as ISO 8859-1 for Western European languages such as English. Do an Internet search for "Extended ASCII codes" for a list of these additional codes and character values.

To consider the relationship between an integer ASCII code value and the character it represents, consider the following program, Char2ASCII. The program accepts a character from the user and displays its ASCII integer equivalent:

```c
#include <stdio.h>
int main()
{
    char c;

    printf("Enter a character to convert to an ASCII code: ");
    scanf("%c",&c);
    printf("The ASCII value of %c = %d\n",c,c);
    return 0;
}
```

Figure E.1 shows three runs of the Char2ASCII program. For the first run, I entered a dollar sign ($), for the second a capital K, and for the last a lowercase k. Using the list of ASCII code and characters shown in Table E.1, you can cross-reference the output from Figure E.1 and see the following is true:

- The integer ASCII value of the $ character is 36.
- The integer ASCII value of the uppercase K character is 75.
- The integer ASCII value of the lowercase k character is 107.

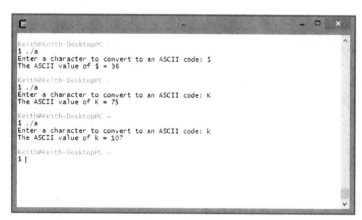

Figure E.1
Three example runs of the Char2ASCII program.

TABLE E.1 COMMON ASCII CHARACTER CODES

Code	Character	Code	Character
0	NUL (null)	30	RS (record separator)
1	SOH (start of heading)	31	US (unit separator)
2	STX (start of text)	32	Space
3	ETX (end of text)	33	!
4	EOT (end of transmission)	34	"
5	ENQ (enquiry)	35	#
6	ACK (acknowledge)	36	$
7	BEL (bell)	37	%
8	BS (backspace)	38	&
9	TAB (horizontal tab)	39	'
10	LF (new line)	40	(
11	VT (vertical tab)	41	)
12	FF (form feed, new page)	42	*
13	CR (carriage return)	43	+
14	SO (shift out)	44	,
15	SI (shift in)	45	–
16	DLE (data link escape)	46	.
17	DC1 (device control 1)	47	/
18	DC2 (device control 2)	48	0
19	DC3 (device control 3)	49	1
20	DC4 (device control 4)	50	2
21	NAK (negative acknowledge)	51	3
22	SYN (synchronous idle)	52	4
23	ETB (end of transmission block)	53	5
24	CAN (cancel)	54	6
25	EM (end of medium)	55	7
26	SUB (substitute)	56	8
27	ESC (escape)	57	9
28	FS (file separator)	58	:
29	GS (group separator)	59	;

TABLE E.1 COMMON ASCII CHARACTER CODES (CONTINUED)

Code	Character	Code	Character
60	<	90	Z
61	=	91	[
62	>	92	\
63	?	93	]
64	@	94	^
65	A	95	–
66	B	96	`
67	C	97	a
68	D	98	b
69	E	99	c
70	F	100	d
71	G	101	e
72	H	102	f
73	I	103	g
74	J	104	h
75	K	105	i
76	L	106	j
77	M	107	k
78	N	108	l
79	O	109	m
80	P	110	n
81	Q	111	o
82	R	112	p
83	S	113	q
84	T	114	r
85	U	115	s
86	V	116	t
87	W	117	u
88	X	118	v
89	Y	119	w

TABLE E.1 COMMON ASCII CHARACTER CODES (CONTINUED)

Code	Character	Code	Character
120	x	124	|
121	y	125	}
122	z	126	~
123	{	127	DEL (Delete)

Common C Library Functions

Tables F.1 through F.6 represent some of the more common C library functions grouped by their corresponding library header file.

TABLE F.1 CTYPE.H

Function Name	Description
isalnum()	Determines if a character is alphanumeric (A–Z, a–z, 0–9)
iscntrl()	Determines if a character is a control (nonprinting) character
isdigit()	Determines if a character is a digit (0–9)
isgraph()	Determines if a character is printable, excluding the space (decimal 32)
islower()	Determines if a character is a lowercase letter (a–z)
isprint()	Determines if a character is printable (decimal 32–126)
ispunct()	Determines if a character is punctuation (decimal 32–47, 58–63, 91–96, 123–126)
isspace()	Determines if a character is white space
isupper()	Determines if a character is an uppercase letter (A–Z)
isxdigit()	Determines if a character is a hex digit (0–9, A–F, a–f)
toupper()	Converts a lowercase character to uppercase
tolower()	Converts an uppercase character to lowercase
isascii()	Determines if the parameter is between 0 and 127
toascii()	Converts a character to American Standard Code for Information Interchange (ASCII)

TABLE F.2 MATH.H

Function Name	Description
acos()	Arccosine
asin()	Arcsine
atan()	Arctangent
atan2()	Arctangent function of two variables
ceil()	Smallest integral value not less than x
cos()	Cosine
cosh()	Hyperbolic cosine
exp()	Exponential
log()	Logarithmic
pow()	Computes a value taken to an exponent
fabs()	Absolute value of floating-point number
floor()	Largest integral value not greater than x
fmod()	Floating-point remainder
frexp()	Converts floating-point number to fractional and integral components
ldexp()	Multiplies floating-point number by integral power of 2
modf()	Extracts signed integral and fractional values from floating-point number
sin()	The sine of an integer
sinh()	Hyperbolic sine
sqrt()	Square root of a number
tan()	Tangent
tanh()	Hyperbolic tangent

TABLE F.3 STDIO.H

Function Name	Description
clearerr()	Clears the end-of-file (EOF) and error indicators
fclose()	Closes a file
feof()	Checks for EOF while reading a file
fflush()	Flushes a stream
fgetc()	Reads a character from a file
fgets()	Reads a record from a file
fopen()	Opens a file for reading or writing
fprintf()	Outputs a line of data to a file
fputc()	Puts a character into a file
fputs()	Puts a string into a file
fread()	Reads data from a stream
freopen()	Opens a file for reading or writing
fseek()	Repositions a file stream
ftell()	Obtains current file position indicator
fwrite()	Writes block of data to a stream
getc()	Retrieves a character from an input stream
getchar()	Retrieves a character from the keyboard (STDIN)
gets()	Retrieves string (from keyboard)
perror()	Prints a system error message
printf()	Outputs data to the screen or a file
putchar()	Outputs a character to STDOUT
puts()	Outputs data to the screen or a file (STDOUT)
remove()	Removes a file
rename()	Renames a file
rewind()	Repositions the file indicator to the beginning of a file
scanf()	Reads formatted data from the keyboard (STDIN)
fscanf()	Reads formatted data from the stream
setbuf()	Provides stream buffering operations
sprintf()	Outputs data in the same way as printf() but puts into a string
sscanf()	Extracts fields from a string
tmpfile()	Creates a temporary file
tmpnam()	Creates a name for a temporary file

TABLE F.4 STDLIB.H

Function Name	Description
abort()	Aborts a program
abs()	Computes the absolute value of an integer
atexit()	Executes the named function when the program terminates
atof()	Converts a string to a double
atoi()	Accepts +-0123456789 leading blanks and converts to integer
atol()	Converts a string to a long integer
bsearch()	Performs a binary search in an array
calloc()	Allocates memory for an array
div()	Computes the quotient and remainder of integer division
exit()	Terminates a program normally
getenv()	Gets an environmental variable
free()	Frees memory allocated with malloc()
labs()	Computes the absolute value of a long integer
ldiv()	Computes the quotient and remainder of long integer division
malloc()	Dynamically allocates memory
mblen()	Determines the number of bytes in a character
mbstowcs()	Converts a multibyte string to a wide character string
mbtowc()	Converts a multibyte character to a wide character
qsort()	Sorts an array
rand()	Generates a random number
realloc()	Reallocates memory
strtod()	Converts a string to a double
strtol()	Converts a string to a long integer
strtoul()	Converts a string to an unsigned long
srand()	Seeds a random number
system()	Issues a command to the operating system
wctomb()	Converts a wide character to a multibyte character
wcstombs()	Converts a wide character string to a multibyte character string

TABLE F.5 STRING.H

Function Name	Description
memchr()	Copies a character into memory
memcmp()	Compares memory locations
memcpy()	Copies n bytes between areas of memory
memmove()	Copies n bytes between areas of potentially overlapping memory
memset()	Sets memory
strcat()	Concatenates two strings
strchr()	Searches for a character in a string
strcmp()	Compares two strings
strcoll()	Compares two strings using the current locale's collating order
strcpy()	Copies a string from one location to another
strcspn()	Searches a string for a set of characters
strerror()	Returns the string representation of an error number
strlen()	Returns the length of a string
strncat()	Concatenates two strings
strncmp()	Compares two strings
strncpy()	Copies part of a string
strpbrk()	Finds characters in a string
strrchr()	Searches for a character in a string
strspn()	Searches a string for a set of characters
strstr()	Searches a string for a substring
strtok()	Parses a string into a sequence of tokens

TABLE F.6 TIME.H

Function Name	Description
asctime()	Converts time to a string
clock()	Returns an approximation of processor time used by the program
ctime()	Converts a time value to string in the same format as asctime()
difftime()	Returns the difference in seconds between two times
gmtime()	Converts time to Coordinated Universal Time (UTC)
localtime()	Converts time to local time
mktime()	Converts time to a time value
strftime()	Formats date and time
time()	Returns time in seconds

Index

Symbols and Numerics

A

W–Z

CPSIA information can be obtained
at www.ICGtesting.com
Printed in the USA
FFOW04n0032170418
46273508-47737FF